ADVANCE PRAISE FOR

Falling Together

"Donna Cardillo shares her personal journey, and the lessons she's learned along the way, authentically and generously. This book will inspire women to practice self-reflection and self-care to discover the profound opportunities and lessons their own lives hold for them too."

—Michelle May, M.D., author of *Eat What You Love, Love What You Eat*

"In this beautiful book, Donna inspires us by telling her life stories of struggle and finding herself, through both common and uncommon journeys of life. Every reader will find moments in the book that their hearts and minds can not only relate to, but feel empowered by hearing Donna's ability to navigate and overcome with grace. The lessons learned at the back of each chapter are particularly inspiring, you will find a gem in each lesson. Definitely a book for every woman."

—Dianne Maroney, RN, MSN; author; founder of The Imagine Project

"I was most touched by the sheer resiliency and determination that is at the heart of Donna Cardillo's life story. No matter what life catapulted her way, she found a way to use her own resources, and those of others, to get through. Even better, the lessons she learned from each challenge embedded themselves within her and moved her successfully forward. Highly recommended for any woman looking to find her way in this journey we call life."

—Flo Schell, EdM; founder: Perceptive Coaching Systems; visionary artist

falling

together

May everything
"fall together"
for you!
Best Wishes —
Donna
Cardillo

Published 2016
Printed in the United States of America
ISBN: 978-1-63152-077-8
Library of Congress Control Number: 015960986

Book design by Stacey Aaronson

For information, address:
She Writes Press
1563 Solano Ave #546
Berkeley, CA 94707

She Writes Press is a division of SparkPoint Studio, LLC.

falling
together

How to Find Balance, Joy,
and Meaningful Change
When Your Life Seems
to Be Falling Apart

DONNA WILK CARDILLO, RN

SHE WRITES PRESS

In memory of my father, Stanley E. Wilk,
the ultimate resilient spirit.

TABLE OF CONTENTS

INTRODUCTION

Sometimes good things have to fall apart
so better things can fall together.
—MARILYN MONROE

EVERY ONE OF US WILL FACE CHALLENGES, CHANGE, AND even a crisis of self at numerous times in our lives. Whether we are faced with illness, divorce, aging, or debilitating low self-esteem, each struggle will offer us a choice: we can fall apart or we can grasp hold of the opportunity to build something new, become more alive, and "fall together" as a new, stronger whole.

It was during one of my most significant life challenges that I first conceived of writing this book. A year and a half earlier, my husband had been diagnosed with a life-altering illness. Inside of the seemingly never-ending devastation, sadness, and grief that followed, I began to notice threads of light reentering my world, reminding me that my life still held beauty and promise. Feeling as though I had crossed a threshold and was now on the other side of darkness, I thought, *Someday I'm going to write a book about this experience.* I wanted to let others who were going through hard times, unexpected life changes, and seemingly insurmountable obstacles know that there is always a way through. But it would take another twenty years, and a lot more living, to bring me to this point. That transition of finding the light again in my own life was just the beginning of my real journey, one that every woman must embark on – the journey to find her own inner warrior, confront her past, and fully embrace her future.

Over the last twenty years as a registered nurse, speaker, columnist, author, seminar and retreat leader, and coach, I've had the privilege of meeting and hearing from thousands of women who have shared their lives' trials and triumphs with me. While doing this work, I became aware that while some women seem to eventually learn to move forward with their lives, embrace change, and even thrive in the face of hardship, others become incapacitated by the same set of circumstances. This both saddened and puzzled me, since the women in the latter group tend to be just as intelligent, passionate, and talented as those in the former group. All had dreams for their futures, but many had given up on themselves and their dreams. I discovered that those women who seemed to struggle the most had simply not yet found the support, resources, inspiration, and information they needed to rise above their challenges, and in some cases move forward with them or in spite of them. I have been both of those women at different times in my life – the one who felt incapacitated and the one who thrived.

Falling Together is about my own process of learning resiliency. It's about my metamorphosis from a woman who was insecure, scared, and self-loathing, into someone who was able to take charge of her life – not by miraculously "solving" all her problems, but by learning to live with them, learn from them, and grow.

I have written this book in the hope that other women will benefit from reading my stories and learning about my path. When we tell our stories we create a sense of community with one another, a bond, a partnership. We share in each other's humanity and join our collective voices to gain strength, wisdom, and insight. As I travel the world sharing my stories and the lessons I've learned with my audiences, women come up to me afterward and say things like:

"Yes, my story is similar."

"You said out loud what I have often thought or felt."

"Thank you for validating my experience."

"I now have a new perspective on my own situation after hearing about your experiences and how you dealt with them."

"I now have the courage to tell my own story."

Over the years I have learned that every woman has a warrior within her, along with unique gifts to bring forward into the world. But often we get derailed on our journey to live an authentic life, one where we come to know ourselves and be true to who we are. My sincere hope is that this book will help you to find courage, inspiration, balance, happiness, and meaningful change in your own life, even when it seems to be falling apart, to continue that journey and light up the world in the process.

chapter one

LOSING SELF

Honor your challenges, for those spaces that you label as dark
are actually there to bring you more light, to strengthen you,
to firm your resolves, and to bring out the best in you.
—SANAYA ROMAN

THE YEAR OF MY FORTIETH BIRTHDAY, I EXPERIENCED WHAT I can only describe as a spiritual crisis. I had a great husband, a nice house, and a supportive family, yet I felt completely lost, confused, and depressed. In other words, I "looked good on paper" to someone on the outside looking in, but I was unhappy with myself and where I was in my life.

For months, I'd been focusing on all the negative aspects of my life and self. I was thinking about all the things I'd done that I wished I hadn't, and all the things I wished I'd done but didn't. Overweight and out of shape, I had developed a frumpy look. I was living in oversized flannel shirts and sweatpants daily. My hair was limp and amorphous, much like my body. I'd been crying almost daily about some past or present hurt or disappointment and withdrawing from social situations. I hadn't gone clothes shopping in several years, so I didn't have anything nice to wear even if I did want to go out. In hindsight, I think it was an excuse to stay isolated: "Gee, I'd love to go with you, but I don't have anything to wear." It was also a symptom of how invisible I felt in my own space. Why pay attention to my appearance when there's nothing to take notice of anyway?

I'm not sure anyone close to me, including my family, noticed or was even paying attention. If they did, no one said anything. I probably got good at hiding my feelings. I was withdrawing into my own dark world.

I wasn't consciously depressed about turning forty. I was, however, aware that those ten-year milestones seem to signal that it's time to take stock. "Am I where I thought I would be at this age?" I asked myself. "Am I where I *want* to be at this age?" I've read that we do first confront our mortality in our forties, and perhaps the birthday reminded me of the passage of time and created a sense of urgency related to the sense that I "wasn't getting any younger."

I remember thinking earlier in my life that women in their forties seemed to be in a good place: experienced, successful in their careers, financially stable, self-assured, and with a sophisticated appearance. I recall looking forward to that decade of life. But while I had amassed some experience and did not have any financial hardships, I certainly didn't look or act like the confident and accomplished woman I had imagined I would be at this age.

When I say I was depressed, I classify it as a spiritual depression as opposed to a bona fide clinical depression, which can be caused by a chemical imbalance, trauma, serious illness, or genetics, and often requires medication and therapy. I don't want to diminish the latter or make light of it. Additionally, while some people use the phrase "spiritual depression" in connection with a crisis of religious faith, that is also not my meaning. I define a spiritual depression as a state of feeling personally lost, confused, unhappy, and even lonely with no obvious resolution. For me it was all that along with a convergence of fears, disappointment, and negativity.

At this point, I'd been married (for the second time) for ten years and had become stepmom to two children who were twenty-four and twenty-six and living on their own. I'd been a registered nurse for almost twenty years, having worked in varied settings, including emergency rooms, psychiatric wards, medical weight control centers, healthcare education companies, and others. But in my mid-thirties, being a nurse had started to drain me. I felt overwhelmed by the sense of being responsible for other people's lives and health. I needed to step back to gain perspective and insight and to simply take a breather. So a couple of years before I fell into this depression, I had left my nursing job to follow an old dream of starting my own antiques business. In addition to doing something I'd long wanted to do, I was able to parlay a passion (collecting antiques) into a small business.

I rented space in a multi-dealer shop where I only

had to show up one day a week to serve as part of the sales team. I could spend the rest of my time doing what I loved most: scouring flea markets, estate sales, and antique shops for hidden treasures and bargains to resell. My husband and I would also set up tables and sell at flea markets and antique shows on the weekends. We both enjoyed interacting with customers, spending time outdoors, and learning more about the items we bought and sold. I was working very hard physically, transporting furniture, lifting heavy boxes of glassware and china, and packing and unpacking the car for shows and markets. My business did provide me with a small income to cover groceries and other minor expenses. But unfortunately, all of my hard work and time spent was not translating into profits that equaled the efforts I was putting forth. By the time I turned forty, I knew that I needed a bigger, better solution for my life and was coming to the end of the line with the antiques business.

Something was about to happen in my life. I could sense it as if it were an impending earthquake, when pressure starts to build up below the earth's surface. Sitting home alone one day in my flannel and fleece, staring out the window and feeling sorry for myself, I suddenly felt as though I was free-falling into a deep, dark hole. I became terrified that if I sank much lower I would be lost forever. In that split second I realized that no one was coming to save me, and that I would have to take action to save my own life. It was like a cosmic alarm clock screaming, "Wake up and get on with your life!" I started taking inventory of where I'd been, where I was now, and where I wanted to go. I knew that I was underutilizing my own potential. I needed to find a way to combine all my talents and experiences to make a bigger difference in the world. I didn't have to think long or hard about what I wanted to do because I'd had an idea, a dream, rolling around in my head for almost ten years: becoming a professional speaker and running public seminars for nurses on nontraditional career opportunities.

The personal crisis that brought my old dream to the surface happened while the healthcare job market was changing dramatically. Nurses were getting laid off from their hospital jobs for the first time in the history of the profession and needed other avenues for employment. So there would never be a better time to bring my seminars forward. I realized that if I didn't do this now, someone else would and I'd be beating myself up over it for the rest of my life. I didn't want to live with regret. I knew that would make me smaller.

Sarah Ban Breathnach, in her classic *Simple Abundance*, refers to this state of restlessness, unhappiness, and emotional pain as "divine discontent," which she likens to "the grit in the oyster before the pearl." In other words, while we typically see this state as something negative and counterproductive, it is actually an energized opportunity to break through the darkness into a more enlightened existence. Many of us hit low points in our lives or careers. I believe they're meant to shock us into action to build a bridge to a better life.

So on that day, desperate to stop my descent into darkness, I made a decision to start my own business and work on becoming a professional speaker. I also made a commitment to do whatever it took to make that business work. If no one came to my first seminars or if they hated them, I would further develop the seminar, or create a new one, market to a different group, or market it in a different way. I decided that failure would not be an option.

I had been repressing the dream because of anxiety and self-doubt about whether or not I could actually accomplish something that seemed so big. It sometimes seems easier or safer to remain ambivalent about important decisions, out of fear of making a "wrong" choice and having to live with the consequences. The way I see it, there are no wrong decisions, only different lessons to learn. Every choice we make has potential pitfalls and rewards. And not doing anything is actually a decision not to act. But after making this decision, I felt energized, focused, and even hopeful. My depression began to lift.

Now that I had made a decision, I was going to need to get pumped up and positive to do the things I was planning, but needed some help. So I took myself down to my local public library in the hopes of finding some inspiration among the books and resources there. Although I hadn't been to the library for a decade or more, I remembered how helpful it had been to me in my younger years while in school. But when I got there, I almost had a panic attack. I was looking for those wooden file boxes with the long narrow drawers and tiny index cards that were used to catalog books. But they were nowhere to be found. Instead there were computers everywhere, and I didn't know how to use a computer! (After all, this was 1993.) I found a friendly looking library staff member and asked for help looking up books. She showed me what I needed to do. Sitting at the computer keyboard, I typed one word into the subject search bar: motivation.

Immediately a list of book titles popped up. Most of them had the same general reference numbers, indicating they were located in the same section. So I found the appropriate aisle (I was a volunteer in a library as a kid, so at least I understood the Dewey decimal system), and with my head tilted to the right so I could read vertically, I began to scan titles with the general gist of *You Can Do It!*, *Get Off Your Butt, Yes You Can!*, and so forth. I immediately started to feel better just reading the titles. I remember thinking, *Hey, maybe there's something to this 'power of positive thinking' theory I've heard about!*

I chose several books that appealed to me and borrowed them to take home. After reading them and doing the writing exercises outlined within, I felt a shift beginning in my mood, my focus, and my outlook. The exercises, which included making a list of my accomplishments to date, recording positive things people had said about me over the years, and writing down favorite motivational quotes, were forcing me (in a good way) to look at myself and my life from a different viewpoint. Rather than dwelling on my perceived shortcomings, as was my natural inclination, I was focusing on my strengths, assets, and achievements. I sensed my depression lifting and my fears becoming background noise rather than the previous deafening clamor. Slowly, my confidence began to build – at least enough to take the next steps necessary to create a business plan. When I focused on the positive that became my reality.

I also began reading biographies of people I admired. A couple that struck a chord were *Miracles Happen*, by Mary Kay Ash, founder of Mary Kay Cosmetics, and *The Story of My Life*, by Helen Keller. Both of these women accomplished great things while overcoming great obstacles. Since I didn't have any major obstacles to overcome just yet (although they were coming), I started to believe that if they could do what they did under duress, surely I could do what I wanted to do under seemingly less harsh circumstances. I didn't realize at the time that their stories would have even more meaning to me when times got tougher over the next few months.

Another book that had a major impact was self-help guru Anthony Robbins's *Awaken the Giant Within*. Even the title got me excited! In this book, Robbins gives the reader permission to see beyond the ordinary to the extraordinary within. After reading it, I listened to the book on CD over and over again until his message really sunk in. He convinced me not only that it was okay to think great thoughts and pursue my dreams, but also that it was what I was supposed to do. Sometimes we have to hear these things from other people. This was propelling me toward my goal and helping to build momentum for the marathon of business ownership.

All of my reading and research led me to the understanding that as humans, we have a natural tendency to focus on the negative. We're hardwired that way. What a relief it was to learn that it isn't just me who has negative thoughts all the time! It's something researchers refer to as the "negativity bias." We tend to fixate on and remember more negative thoughts and images than positive ones. We have tapes playing in our heads telling us why we can't do something or reminding us of our perceived shortcomings. Unfortunately, there's no "off" button on those tapes. But you can turn down the volume on the negative thoughts while turning up the volume on the positive ones. Each of us has to work to get and stay positive and motivated. It doesn't come easily to most people, including myself. I knew I would have to work hard to neutralize the naturally occurring dissenting voices in my head.

Another powerful, effective way I discovered to do this is to spend time with others who are positive, supportive, and motivated. Many of us spend our days with people who are dead of spirit, motivation, and hope for the future. Sometimes it's coworkers – or even worse, friends and family. So it's important to get out among "the living" and seek out upbeat, encouraging, optimistic people who are doing the kinds of things you'd like to do.

If left to our own devices and negative thought patterns, many of us would simply sink into oblivion, as I had been about to do that day at home. I found these role models, mentors, and kindred spirits through professional associations such as the National Association of Women Business Owners, the National Speakers Association, and the American Nurses Association, as well as through word-of-mouth networking. I joined these organizations, attended meetings and networking events, and made telephone and face-to-face appointments when possible with those I wished to emulate and learn from. I asked them to share their best advice and success tips with me, which they very graciously did.

During the following year and a half, I read voraciously, spent an increasing amount of time in area libraries, interviewed other speakers, nurses, and business owners, and formulated my seminar and workbook for my first big gigs. That one big decision – to become a speaker and start a seminar business – was like a match lighting a stick of dynamite. Inactivity turned to activity, apathy turned to enthusiasm, and lethargy turned to energy. Decisions create action, and action creates results. For me, it was a perfect illustration of how a well-thought-out decision, even one that dares to assume some risk, is a powerful force. I continued to gain energy and focus, was paying more attention to my appearance, and was slowly getting back out into the world.

In the spring of 1995, I was finally ready to schedule my first seminars for autumn of that year. This would require contacting New Jersey hotels (I had decided to stay local for now) in different cities for meeting space, designing brochures, and creating a marketing plan. Everything was on schedule and the excitement was building. But just as I was rejoicing at having found myself and my path, I was about to lose my bearings once again.

After years of working in the corporate world, my husband, Joe, had recently made a transition into selling real estate. One Saturday afternoon in April, Joe came home from the office and told me that while working on the computer he'd had an episode where his hands and lower arms suddenly went numb and he couldn't use them. It lasted a few minutes, but feeling and then function had eventually returned. He seemed quietly concerned, but was trying not to get too worked up about it.

As an RN, I didn't know what was wrong with him, but my gut told me it was something serious. We immediately went to our family doctor to have him checked out. For some unknown reason, I opted not to go into the exam room with him as I normally would. I must have been subconsciously afraid of what the physician would find. I stayed in the waiting room, perched nervously on the front half of a black institutional plastic chair, like a child waiting to be called into the principal's office. When my husband came out to the waiting room he explained, in a very neutral tone, that the doctor was sending him for an MRI of the brain. I don't remember feeling anything at that point. I think I was just waiting for a cue from someone, anyone, to dictate what my next move should have been. So much felt out of my control. I needed an anchor, a focus, to keep me steady, such as a task that I could execute. MRI needed? I'll take care of that.

I went up to the receptionist's desk to get the referral form while she was on the phone with the MRI facility calling in the order. While I was standing there, I noticed an X-ray form with my husband's name on it and a diagnosis of "left hemiparesis," which means left-sided weakness. I angrily stated to the receptionist, while she was still on the telephone, that the diagnosis was wrong. I assumed someone had written that on the wrong form since, other than that brief episode at the real estate office, Joe had no lingering disability. To add to my frustration, she was trying to pronounce the word "hemi-paresis" to the X-ray facility, and she couldn't get it out. She kept sputtering, "hem-eee . . . hem-eee," and I would bark at her, "Hem-eee-par-eee-sis . . . Hem-eee-par-eee-sis!" My mounting agitation and impatience was my denial (and escalating fear) of what was actually going on.

Of course the diagnosis on the form was correct. Upon examination, the physician had detected that my husband had left-sided weakness, something neither of us was aware of because it was not profound. He had been having some challenges with flexibility and seemed to be tripping a lot, but his father used to shuffle his feet, and I assumed it was an inherited trait. Joe was fifty-two years old at this time.

After getting the MRI, we went to see a neurologist as instructed. The waiting room was tiny and no one in the office, including the doctor, smiled. Perhaps they were accustomed to doling out bad news and had all acquired a serious demeanor. It added to the heaviness of the situation. On that first visit, the physician told us there were areas of white shadows on my husband's brain and that further tests would be needed to determine the cause. She said she was quite sure it wasn't a stroke but didn't yet know for sure what is was. As a nurse, I needed more information and asked her, "What are the possibilities?" She rattled off nonchalantly, as if reading a grocery list aloud, that it could be brain cancer, Lou Gehrig's disease (ALS), multiple sclerosis, or Lyme disease – but she quickly added that she didn't think it was Lyme disease. My husband and I sat there in utter shock and horror. Brain cancer? Lou Gehrig's disease? Multiple sclerosis? And if there could be one thing that was the lesser of the evils on that list – Lyme disease – she was quite sure it wasn't that.

It's hard to explain that moment in time when you realize that your life and the life of a loved one are inalterably changed by serious illness. It's as if everything in the world drops away, like when you use the zoom lens on a camera, this one thing comes into sharp focus and is magnified tenfold. It's all you see, even though you don't know exactly what you're looking at.

Joe and I left the office and silently went to our car. I went into nurse mode and started making arrangements for the next set of tests: spinal tap, blood work, more X-rays. In the meantime, Joe's walking seemed to deteriorate almost immediately. Within days of the office visit, he started to limp. I recall observing him hobble to his car from the house, and it was emotionally painful to watch. What had happened to the strong, energetic, athletic man I knew? Like thumbing through a child's flipbook, I felt I was watching him slip away from me in stop motion, page by page.

On a follow-up visit to the neurologist, which Joe went to on his own because I had a prior commitment (again, I think I was in denial or afraid to hear the final verdict), she told him that her final diagnosis was multiple sclerosis (MS). Because there are no definitive tests to come to this conclusion, and a diagnosis is usually made by eliminating other possibilities, we decided to visit an MS specialist for a second opinion. He confirmed the diagnosis. At least we weren't living with the fear of something that might take his life in the near future like cancer or ALS, whatever little comfort that provided. We now had a new reality – one that seemed horrifying and unfathomable. Our previous life and future plans – so many things we all take for granted every day – had completely evaporated.

MS is a neurological autoimmune disorder in which the body attacks the coating (myelin) around the nervous system. This can cause a variety of symptoms including diminished coordination, muscle spasticity and weakness, debilitating fatigue, and poor cognitive function. The disease is very unpredictable and affects everyone differently. Joe has what is known as secondary progressive

MS. This means that he has a steadily progressing form of the illness rather than the relapsing/remitting type that is more common. More than anything, the illness immediately affected his ability to walk. Over the next ten years he progressed to relying on a cane, then a walker, and eventually a wheelchair. One of the great challenges with MS is that the cause is not known; therefore, therapies are aimed primarily at symptom management. Many of the so-called treatments, primarily injectable and intravenous medications, are marginally effective at best and carry their own set of serious side effects.

Soon after the diagnosis, Joe began to withdraw into himself and get clinically depressed. To make matters even worse, he developed a huge lump on his neck that grew to the size of an ostrich egg. It turned out to be an infected lymph gland, which was treatable and subsided in a few weeks. But what else would go wrong? Our world suddenly seemed like Dorothy's house in *The Wizard of Oz*, being yanked from its roots by the tornado and hurled into a strange and scary place.

As if in a trance, I pushed myself through each day. I couldn't help wondering what life would be like now and in the future. What would happen to Joe and the life we had planned? These were questions that had to be faced . . . addressed . . . but there were no answers. Among the biggest questions in my mind was whether or not to go forward with my business plan. Because I had not yet invested much money into the business or actually scheduled any seminars, I considered completely scrapping my plans and looking for a more traditional job that would provide a regular paycheck and benefits. Since my business would require me to travel, I questioned how Joe would manage while I was on the road if his disability progressed much further. I had to do some soul searching and decided to take some time to reflect on everything. Fortunately, Joe was willing to go along with whatever I decided, although I know he was nervous about the risks of business ownership.

After two weeks of mulling things over while going through the routine of daily life, I came to the decision that I would move forward with my business plan based on the following:

1. In six months' time, Joe might be significantly incapacitated, or he could still be somewhat mobile and independent. There was no way to know. In fact, none of us know what the future holds. So I made my decision based on where we were then, rather than on where we might be down the road. If circumstances changed, then we would find another way, make adjustments, or modify our plan. Isn't that how life is anyway?

2. I could get a traditional job, but there was no guarantee that I wouldn't get laid off in six months or a year like so many others in the volatile and changing job market of the mid-1990s. So there was no real security in that

path. I believed that in the long run, my family and I would be better off if I relied on myself rather than an employer to financially support us.

3. If I didn't pursue this dream, I feared I would always regret it and wonder "what if?" It is said that when people are on their deathbeds, they don't regret the things they did, but rather the things they didn't do. And I didn't want to resent Joe or get bitter.

So I launched my first public seminar, titled Career Alternatives for Nurses, in September 1995 at a Holiday Inn in Toms River, New Jersey. Twenty-five nurses attended, and I wanted to kiss and hug every single one of them, but refrained. No one walked out during my six-hour presentation, and I considered that in itself a success. I felt a great sense of relief and accomplishment at the end of the day and was now looking forward to the additional five seminars I had scheduled in the coming months.

So here I was, a proud new business owner, learning and growing each day while fulfilling a longtime dream. There was so much work to do to keep the momentum going and create something sustainable. But while I had just successfully found myself as a business owner, I was also, unbeknownst to me, about to lose myself again in the role of caretaker. From the onset of Joe's illness, I began taking on more and more of the physical and emotional responsibilities of our lives, our home, and our family. Not only was he less able to do physical work, such as mowing the grass or running errands, but he was becoming emotionally detached from his life – and that included me. He would spend hours playing solitaire on the computer and didn't seem to have much interest in or patience for things I wanted to discuss with him. We were still married, but I began to feel like I was living my life as a single woman.

To fuel my growing sense of isolation and over-whelm, I did not always feel supported by some of the people close to us. Family members and friends, who would greet Joe in a very upbeat way, smiling, patting him on the back, and telling him how great he looked, would then corner me in a private place and ask in an ominous tone about how he was "really" doing. At times, I felt as though I was being ambushed. I remember some-one close to us approaching me at a family function and not even greeting me but instead sternly confronting me about the state of our healthcare insurance (we were both self-employed at that time, and this person was concerned that we might not be covered). I assured this person that we had insurance and intended to keep it up, so there was nothing to worry about. Another family member later told me that this person had remarked how rude I was for saying not to worry. I felt like I was getting it from all angles.

Another time, some close friends we hadn't seen in several months came to visit. Everyone seemed happy and was having a good time. When my girlfriend got me alone in the kitchen, she broke down sobbing and was inconsolable, so much so that she couldn't speak for a few minutes. I wondered what was wrong, thinking she had bad news to tell me about herself or her family. I kept thinking, Who died? When she finally was able to speak, she expressed how sad and upset she was about Joe's worsening disability (he had progressed to walking with a cane at this point). Despite being taken aback to learn that her extreme emotional distress was about Joe, I had to comfort and console her. But who would console me? I had become family spokesperson, provider of medical updates, therapist, bearer of others' depression and concern, and even chief comforter. I was on a path to burnout as I once again started feeling lost, this time because I was being swallowed whole by my caregiving duties.

There were also a few friends who distanced themselves from us or cut themselves off entirely. This is an all-too-common story when serious illnesses or family challenges strike. I had experienced something similar when I went through my divorce years earlier. Some people just can't cope with what's happening in your life and perhaps don't know how to relate or what to say. I think in some cases it is a form of denial of life's harsh realities and a way for them to reinforce in their minds, "This will never happen to me."

In order to learn more about Joe's illness and find support, we got involved with our local chapter of the National Multiple Sclerosis Society (NMSS) and attended educational programs for those newly diagnosed. I kept hearing the word "caregiver" in relation to those of us who did not have MS but "cared for" someone who did. I rejected the word and the notion entirely as it did not apply to me, or so I thought. After all, Joe did not yet need help bathing, eating, or dressing. And that was, to me, what caregiving meant. And even though as a registered nurse I know that nursing care covers all aspects of a person's physical, emotional, and spiritual well-being, I just didn't see things that way in my personal life.

Thank goodness for the Internet because while researching information about MS, I happened upon the website of the National Family Caregivers Association (now the Caregiver Action Network). Though it was started by a woman whose husband had MS, it is for all family caregivers. As I read through page after page describing all the things that I was doing (taking on more emotional responsibility, running to medical appointments, doing more of the physical work at home, picking up prescriptions, and so on – all things I hadn't considered caregiving), I finally recognized and accepted that I was indeed a caregiver or "carepartner." I learned that not only was I entitled to care and support for myself, but that it was actually vital for my health and safety as well as my husband's. I wanted to cry. Finally I'd found insight and validation for what I was experiencing. Someone was telling my story in the universal sense.

But while that affirmation was important, I still felt

increasingly isolated and stressed. Local resources for caregivers were sparse at the time, so I finally decided to start my own self-help group (because I didn't already have enough to do!) for family and friends of people with MS. And although initially it was good to connect with others, the group members began to look to me for comfort, information, and support. So rather than being nurtured and supported, I was once again in the role of caregiver to these group members, and I could not continue to do that. I felt that I was being eaten alive.

When people are desperate, whether for information, comfort, or help of some kind, they will cling to whatever is available to them. In this case, it was me they were clinging to. After a grueling year or so of monthly meetings, I left the group. Things were getting so intense for me, there were days that I wondered if I would be able to continue to run a business and be a family caregiver at the same time. However, I had no intention of giving the business up, and obviously my caregiving duties were not only not going to go away, but would likely expand as time went on. I felt like a pressure cooker left too long on the stove, ready to blow.

In the end it was Joe himself who pointed me in the direction of the healing I needed by setting a positive example in a decision he made to seek professional help for himself. Our local chapter of NMSS offered two free counseling sessions with a clinical social worker, and Joe decided to take advantage of that. I admire him so much for having the courage to take that step. Many people resist getting the help and support they need in times of crisis and major life changes. Some see seeking professional help as a sign of weakness. In reality, it's a sign of strength.

Our insurance company covered future sessions, and Joe continued on with the counselor. We went together on occasion, and I eventually went by myself. We were both dealing with so many emotions and changes individually and in our relationship, I don't know that we could have sorted it all out on our own.

Many marriages break up when one partner is diagnosed with a serious illness. I can understand why that happens. Both partners are suffering, each in his and her own way, and often unable to comfort or support one another. This can result in neither party's needs being met, which is a recipe for relationship disaster. Both Joe and I were keeping many feelings to ourselves prior to seeing the counselor. For example, he felt that he was becoming less of a man because of his illness and was afraid that I might fall out of love with him. He also resented needing more help with things and was directing much of his anger toward me. I felt that I was being taken for granted and unappreciated for all the things I was doing, in spite of the increasing burden of caregiving I was carrying. As a result, we were snapping at each other, angry much of the time, and bickering over little things, which made daily life very unpleasant. Ongoing counseling helped us to communicate better; confront the tough issues in a safe, mediated setting; address our related grief and loss issues; and deal with our own individual challenges.

The first time I went to see the therapist alone, as soon as the door closed behind me I started to sob – that uncontrollable, can't-catch-your-breath, primal, body-jerking wail of one who is experiencing deep emotional pain and loss. The therapist, a slight, studious-looking woman probably in her forties, motioned for me to sit down while I continued to cry. She seemed completely unfazed by my emotional outburst, as if she had seen it a thousand times before. This went on for about ten minutes until my tear ducts dried up. I finally had a safe place to let it all out, and let it out I did. I had been putting on my game face for my husband and our family and friends for so long. I was holding it together for everyone else. I knew that if I internalized my deep sadness, fear, and sense of overwhelm for much longer, I would break down either emotionally or physically. I still see a counselor periodically when life gets overwhelming, and I have an occasional good cry behind those safe closed doors. I consider it routine maintenance for life.

This same therapist shared with us, at a group educational session, a piece titled "Welcome to Holland." It was written by a woman after she had a child with Down syndrome. It beautifully illustrates the positive shift in perspective that can occur when you find yourself somewhere other than where you originally set out to go.

WELCOME TO HOLLAND

by

Emily Perl Kingsley

I am often asked to describe the experience of raising a child with a disability — to try to help people who have not shared that unique experience to understand it, to imagine how it would feel. It's like this . . .

When you're going to have a baby, it's like planning a fabulous vacation trip — to Italy. You buy a bunch of guide books and make your wonderful plans. The Coliseum. The Michelangelo David. The gondolas in Venice. You may learn some handy phrases in Italian. It's all very exciting.

After months of eager anticipation, the day finally arrives. You pack your bags and off you go. Several hours later, the plane lands. The flight attendant comes in and says, "Welcome to Holland."

"Holland?!?" you say. "What do you mean Holland?? I signed up for Italy! I'm supposed to be in Italy. All my life I've dreamed of going to Italy."

But there's been a change in the flight plan. They've landed in Holland and there you must stay.

The important thing is that they haven't taken you to a horrible, disgusting, filthy place, full of pestilence, famine and disease. It's just a different place.

So you must go out and buy new guide books. And you must learn a whole new language. And you will meet a whole new group of people you would never have met.

It's just a different place. It's slower-paced than Italy, less flashy than Italy. But after you've been there for a while and you catch your breath, you look around . . . and you begin to notice that Holland has windmills . . . and Holland has tulips. Holland even has Rembrandts.

But everyone you know is busy coming and going from Italy . . . and they're all bragging about what a wonderful time they had there. And for the rest of your life, you will say, "Yes, that's where I was supposed to go. That's what I had planned."

And the pain of that will never, ever, ever, ever go away . . . because the loss of that dream is a very very significant loss.

But . . . if you spend your life mourning the fact that you didn't get to Italy, you may never be free to enjoy the very special, the very lovely things . . . about Holland.

∽

I seem to recall feeling angry about this piece when it was first presented to us. It came across like an attempt to put a sugar coating on something very distasteful. How could anyone find something positive in something so devastating and life altering, and suggest that a simple shift in outlook would do the trick? And how dare someone challenge my rejection of this new frightening place I found myself in, which I wanted nothing to do with? But in time, and with the help of the therapist and my own self-work, I came to understand Kingsley's words and her perspective. She meant that although there is initially disappointment and shock about not landing where you set out to go, there were wonderful opportunities and joys available where you wind up. But you won't be able to embrace your new location and all the gifts it offers you if you only focus on where you originally thought you'd be. This scenario would eventually play itself out in my own life.

For the first eighteen months after Joe's diagnosis, my world felt dark, heavy, and thick with confusion, shock, helplessness, fear, and grief. It was like walking through a smoke cloud, coughing and choking every step of the way, eyes burning, and getting light-headed from lack of oxygen. But you can only go on so long that way before it takes an irreparable toll on you. Once again, as when I turned forty, I found myself disoriented, anxious, and lost. I couldn't believe the two extremes I was experiencing: my business was one of the most exciting things that had ever happened to me, and Joe's illness one of the most devastating. Was the universe trying to temper both of them for me? Or perhaps it was some cruel practical joke. And while a goal and related action plan had pulled me through the depression I experienced at age forty, something even more powerful and challenging would be needed to pull me through this melancholy – a change in perspective.

When I was at the point of not knowing how much longer I could stay on in the smoke cloud described above, something shifted. One bright, sunny autumn morning, I was sitting in my kitchen, gazing into my wooded backyard with the bright seasonal colors of the changing leaves. I was watching the birds flit and fly around the birdfeeder, the squirrels jump up on the birdbath to quench their thirst, and the bunnies hop around, nibbling the grass. Suddenly it struck me that, although my world seemed to be in suspended animation, life was still going on actively all around me. I felt bathed in a warm, soothing light reminding me that in spite of our struggles, the sun continued to rise and set each day, there were still things in life to celebrate and cherish, and my family still needed me. I decided it was time to stop being sad and angry and resisting what is, to stop wishing for things to go back to the way they had been, and instead to embrace and accept my new location and make the best of it, whatever that might look like. Things had permanently changed in our lives, and we would not be returning to where we once were. I needed to find a new rhythm of life – a "new normal," as I like to call it. Just as when I had to make a decision about whether or not to start my business in spite of obvious challenges, once again I was choosing to move forward rather than stay stagnant.

When I first used that phrase, "new normal," my husband defensively said, "There is nothing normal about this situation." But I explained that I saw it as our new reality, like it or not, and that we were going to need to find ways to work with it, and in some cases, around it. As I said the words, I had a sense of finding myself again, and claiming my place in this changing landscape.

That's when the black cloud that had hovered over me for a year and a half began to lift, and the sunlight started to stream back into my life, just as it had that morning through my kitchen windows. I felt as though I had made it to the other side of darkness. Working toward acceptance, the acknowledgment of reality, allowed me to deal with it and let the light come in again. I've seen others use resistance or denial ("Why me?" or "This can't be happening to me.") in facing similar situations. This approach, if prolonged, creates unnecessary suffering and darkness.

Over time, as Joe and I began to learn the steps to a new dance, our counselor inquired if we would like to present as a couple at future programs for those newly diagnosed with MS. We were asked to talk about changes in our relationship and family structure, such as shifting roles and responsibilities, how we learned to nurture and respect each other in a new way, and in general how we were learning to cope with a "new normal." The thought of turning something so seemingly horrible into something potentially positive (being able to use our own struggles to help others) was appealing to us both. So we agreed to become regular presenters at these events and came to look forward to the opportunity to share our experiences. We were even able to inject some humor into our "act," which we eventually referred to as the "Joe and Donna Show." We found ways to convey to others, and in so doing, to ourselves that there is life after a diagnosis of MS (or any other debilitating illness), and that life can be full, beautiful, rewarding, and yes – even fun. Theologian Desiderius Erasmus said, "Give light and the darkness will disappear of itself."

One of the things about serious illness is that it forces us to focus on what is really important in our lives. When you suddenly lose so much that you once took for granted, you grow to appreciate what you do have – or at least you have that opportunity. There is beauty, wealth of all kinds, and sacredness everywhere, as Emily Kingsley points out, if you look for it. In fact, some people have referred to this as "the gift" of serious illness or disability. So many of us get bogged down with unimportant things, or waste time and energy on resentment, anger, and pettiness. We are given this life, and it is our choice how we live it.

Joe had spent the first year after his diagnosis focusing on his losses. He eventually came to realize that there were still things that he *could* do, and actually *loved* to do, but had gotten away from. These include painting in oils and preparing gourmet meals – two things he's exceptionally good at. And while he previously had little time for these activities, because of his forced retirement due to his disability he now had all the time in the world to indulge in his passions!

For me, Joe's illness was a wakeup call. It reminded me of how precious and fragile life and the ones we love are. When Joe and I have really scary and bad days, weeks, and even years, we always remind each other of these gifts and refocus on what is really important in our lives: family, each other, good friends. Additionally, I started to be consciously grateful for so many things I had previously taken for granted: being able to take a deep breath, the ability to walk unencumbered, a roof over our heads, food in the cupboard, and the opportunity to have one more day to contribute something to the world. I also realized that I am never alone. There are always people somewhere, whether professionals, family, friends, or even sometimes strangers, who become friends when I ask for and accept help and support, something that has never been easy for me.

So what does "normal" look like for us, twenty years after Joe's MS diagnosis and the launching of my first seminar? It involves more time and planning when doing simple things like getting in and out of the car, eating meals, and getting both of us ready in the morning. It includes having special equipment in the house such as wheelchairs, walkers, and canes. When at the mall or food store, you might see Joe cruising along in his motorized scooter, beeping at anyone moving slower than him (often elderly people), and me pretending I don't know him when he does so. If you drive by my house, you're likely to see our teenage grandson tooling around the yard in Joe's scooter and the younger grandson propelling himself around in Joe's spare wheelchair, popping wheelies when he thinks we're not watching. Since their grandpa has been disabled for their entire lives, this is all normal to them. They respect the equipment, have been shown how to use it properly, and know to ask permission first. And while the mere sight of a wheelchair depresses some people, to two boys fascinated by anything with wheels or a motor, these vehicles are just cool stuff to play with at our house. It's all a matter of perspective.

As it turns out, moving forward with the business was the right decision for me and for us. Although we struggled emotionally and financially for several years, today we are in a better place than we likely would have been otherwise. One of the unexpected benefits is that because I can work from home when I am not traveling, and Joe is now retired, we spend more time together than we did our entire pre-diagnosis married life, which is such a blessing. And I am more available to help him on a day-to-day basis. Additionally, I have more freedom and flexibility in my life than I ever had before. Having my own business allows me to make my own schedule, so I can carve out time, as needed, for my other immediate family members – parents, grown children, grandchildren, and even myself.

Starting this business also saved me emotionally. Because it required so much of my time, thought process, and emotional energy during that start-up phase, it was the only way I could truly "escape" for a few moments or hours from the horror of what was happening in our lives at that time and the pain of watching my husband suffer. I was able to throw myself into it, and it offered me brief respite. As a result of starting my business, I have grown beyond anything I could have anticipated. I have become emotionally stronger, more confident, and more resilient. Dealing with Joe's illness and disability at the same time has made me more compassionate and patient, which in turn makes me a better business owner and better human being. Because I share many of my own struggles in my writing and speaking, the women I work with know that I can relate to their struggles. And even though I have better coping strategies today than I did twenty years ago, the rewards, adventures, and even the challenges of business ownership and pursuing my own dreams allow me to maintain a sense of independence and self-awareness so I don't lose myself again.

So what does "losing oneself" really mean? It is a point where we become disconnected from our true selves: our likes, our interests, our talents, our joys. At age forty, I was working in the antiques business, which was not intellectually challenging or stimulating to me. I wasn't stretching myself or learning anything of substance. I'd let my appearance go and was staying somewhat isolated, making me almost invisible. I had stepped away from healthcare and the role of the healer that is so integral to who I am. I had lost a connection with my true, authentic self. Fortunately, my attempts to work through that, including making a big decision, setting a goal, and taking action steps in the face of great obstacles, led me down the road to self-discovery. I eventually "found" myself and my path just beyond the boundaries of my comfort zone, where I now permanently reside.

When Joe got sick, I was sucked into the vortex of caregiving without even realizing it at first. And although I was running my business then and challenged and growing in that way, I was caring for everyone else except me, and lost myself once again. The same thing happens with many women who get disconnected from or lose who they are by focusing too much on others without nurturing themselves, whether in the role of caregiver, mother, or partner. This also happens when they are living a life that they or someone else thought they "should," rather than the one they would choose for themselves.

After twenty years of traveling the world speaking and having the privilege of meeting many people who have shared their stories and struggles with me, I've learned that everyone is carrying a heavy load and facing challenges, many of them very significant. When I hear from women who seem to be lost like I was, I encourage them to start doing simple things that bring them back to themselves, things that give them joy, that feed their creative side, that nurture their bodies and souls. I also tell them that it is never too late to follow their dreams, no matter what else is going on in their life. In fact, creating and preserving your own slice of life, something just for you, is vital to your personal growth, health, and happiness. Each of us has a story to tell and hurdles to overcome. But we become stronger and more ourselves by acting rather than hesitating.

LESSONS LEARNED

1. Sometimes you have to lose yourself before you can truly find yourself.

2. Don't wait for circumstances to be perfect before moving forward in your life; they never will be. And so much can happen while you're waiting. Live your life while you have the chance. No one's path is smooth or without obstacles.

3. Many of us hit low points in our life/career. They are meant to shock us into action to build a bridge to a better life.

4. When you focus on the positive, that will become your reality.

5. There are no wrong decisions, only different lessons to learn.

6. Decisions create action, and action creates results. A well-thought-out decision, even one that dares to assume some risk, is a powerful force.

7. Seeking professional help if needed in times of crisis and major change is a sign of strength.

8. Helping others and being proactive is a great way to deal with grief, pain, and loss.

9. Life's path may not take you where you set out to go, but you can still enjoy the scenery and even the new destination.

10. We become strong and more alive by acting rather than hesitating.

RECOMMENDED READING

Canfield, Jack, and Janet Switzer. *The Success Principles: How to Get from Where You Are to Where You Want to Be.* New York: HarperCollins, 2005.

Kushner, Harold S. *When Bad Things Happen to Good People.* New York: Schocken Books, 2001. First published 1981.

Sheehy, Gail. *Passages in Caregiving: Turning Chaos into Confidence.* New York: William Morrow, 2010.

RESOURCES

National Association of Women Business Owners www.nawbo.org

Caregiver Action Network www.caregiveraction.org

Well Spouse Association www.wellspouse.org

www.mentalhelp.net/selfhelp

chapter two

LOVE LOST AND FOUND

Lovers don't finally meet somewhere.
They exist in each other all along.

—RUMI

I ALWAYS TELL MY HUSBAND JOE THAT I LOVED HIM LONG before I met him. For as long as I can remember, I believed in my heart that someday I would meet the love of my life. I had a sense of "knowing" this person without having yet met him. I didn't imagine a certain look or even attributes, but, corny as it sounds, I felt I had a soul connection with someone out there.

There's a Rascal Flatts song with a lyric: *I know God blessed the broken road / That led me straight to you.* The song poeticizes the belief that past disappointments and heartaches were all part of a grander plan leading to a true love. How that theme describes our coming together, including all that preceded it! I had considerable growing up to do and some painful lessons in love and marriage to learn in a previous relationship before I would be ready to offer my best self to Joe. But the story starts even before my first marriage.

During my teenage years I swore I would never get married. I was determined to live an unconventional life and didn't want to be tied down. I saw women getting married and having children and keeping house and wanted none of that. I did want to travel, be free to make my own decisions, and be financially independent. I counted the days until I would finish nursing school, move out of my parents' house, and get my own place.

By my early twenties, I was a registered nurse living in the borough of New Milford, in my home state of New Jersey. I was renting a sunny little second-floor apartment in a garden complex, which I could barely afford. But I was blissfully happy to be on my own with no one to answer to and no one to be responsible for. I had a job that I loved, working in the emergency room of a community hospital – the same one I had worked in as a student nurse, so I already had a sense of belonging there. It seemed my dreams of independence were coming true.

A patient who regularly visited the outpatient clinic connected to the ER where I worked, and was a self-proclaimed psychic, came in one day and said she kept "seeing" an engagement ring on my finger. She told me I would be getting married soon. I told her in no uncertain terms that there was no way that was going to happen. Later that day, I laughed as I told my coworkers about her "prediction." Yet that very evening, I ran into the man who would become husband number one.

After work, a group of friends and I went into a local hangout where hospital staff congregated. Dan (not his real name) was sitting at the bar talking with a guy friend, and I had to walk right past him. Although we'd never officially been introduced, I knew that he was a psychiatric orderly at the hospital. I would see him going through the ER, taking his patients for outside walks. On one occasion when I just happened to be in the hallway as he was passing through, he had stopped to ask me about the straight line on the paper in the EKG machine we kept in the hallway. I explained that we always ran what we called a "blank strip" after each electrocardiogram, thus the straight line. He said he was relieved because he always assumed that meant someone had died. He was a little taller than me, had long hair and a moustache, and wore big glasses; in short, he was a bit of a hippie. But he had a friendly face and smile, and I thought he was attractive. So when I passed him in the bar that night, I lightly touched his arm, introduced myself, and relayed that I remembered his asking me about the EKG strip.

He seemed delighted that I remembered that, even though he didn't necessarily remember my being the person he spoke with. He told me at a later time that the fact I touched his arm gave him a good feeling about me. We started to talk and continued our conversation until the bar was closing. He seemed intelligent and interesting and had a good sense of humor. I can't remember what we spoke about, but it felt relaxed and enjoyable. I invited him to my place for coffee so we could continue the conversation, which lasted until dawn. We both had to go to work that day, so we had to part company, but he asked if I'd like to go out later that week and I agreed. We began spending more time together and quickly became inseparable. He had been living in a house in New Jersey that his parents owned, though they had since moved to Florida. When they decided to sell the house, about ten months after we started dating, he needed to find a new place to live. We talked it over and it just seemed to make sense for him to move in with me.

About a year after our cohabitation began, we mutually decided to get married, not by proposal but by discussion. It seemed more like a practical next step rather than some romantic notion of spending the rest of our lives together. Though I'd always held out the idea of myself as unmarried and free, I was now tired of being single, with the associated loneliness, and thought marriage might provide some security or stability in my life. Plus, I wanted to buy a house and on some level believed that the only respectable way to do that while cohabiting with someone of the opposite sex was to get hitched. I was sure that's what my parents would think, and I had a deep-seated need to get their approval and their blessing on the whole arrangement.

But even though I had agreed to get married, I still had a subconscious aversion to the whole concept, so I did everything I could to keep the process low-key. In hindsight, I seemed to need to neutralize it or maintain some sort of denial to minimize the appearance of a wedding. I had what I now call an "un-wedding." I bought a twenty-dollar ivory-colored dress off the rack (on sale, of course) in a regular clothing store, hardly invited any family members, but did invite my friends, for a total of about fifty people. I approached it more like a big party rather than a wedding reception. We got married by the mayor in an Elks hall and hired a coworker's father's band to provide some music. I can't even remember if we exchanged rings or not. Talk about blocking! The year was 1977. I was twenty-four and Dan was twenty-six.

Nor did the wedding ceremony put an end to my nagging ambivalence about being married. When I returned to work, having legally changed my last name to his (as unconventional as I liked to fancy myself, I am really very conventional in many ways), I would answer the phone, stating my name and purposely muffling my new last name so it wouldn't be obvious to others that I was now married. I'm sure Freud would have a field day with that. And just to give you some insight into how the marriage started off, on our honeymoon, after driving from New Jersey to a motel in Colonial Williamsburg, Virginia – a state that claims to be for lovers – my new husband was complaining about everything and in such a bad mood that when we checked into our "honeymoon" room, I threw myself on the bed and cried my eyes out. I'd known that he could be cranky at times, but I was taken aback that he could find it in himself to be in such a foul mood on such a supposedly joyous occasion. We enjoyed some sightseeing during the week but shared no physical intimacy. It turned out the honeymoon would be a good predictor of things to come.

Back in New Jersey, we settled into the routine of our new life together. After continuing to live briefly in my garden apartment, we bought a beautiful old colonial house in Maplewood, New Jersey, the town I had grown up in and where my parents and sister still lived. After having been so eager to create some space between myself and my family after getting out of nursing school (my apartment was about an hour away from my hometown), I apparently felt the need for some renewed geographic closeness. So I got my house and my husband and I settled into what seemed like a tolerable life. At least I wasn't alone. However, one can still be lonely even with other people around – but I found ways to avoid thinking about that.

We were both getting our careers into high gear, he as a sales rep for a technical school and I as a manager for a medical weight-control center, so I focused on that area of my life that was going well. We argued regularly about money from the start. I was trying to live within our meager means, while he had no problem running up our credit cards to the max on things like tools and woodworking machinery that he barely used. I was in charge of the checkbook and paying the bills and didn't want to incur any debt. By contrast, he wanted to only make minimum payments on our mounting arrears and didn't care about the accruing interest. I remember him telling me regularly and emphatically, "I want more cash in my pocket!" To him it seemed that buying things on credit and being in no hurry to pay for them was a way to do this. It was making me increasingly anxious and unhappy.

To make matters worse, he seemed suddenly uncomfortable spending time with my family or friends after we got married, and even with our neighbors when they invited us over. We lived across the street from a lovely couple whom I often chatted with outside. The wife asked if we would come over for drinks sometime. When I told Dan, he stated flatly that he was not going. He wouldn't give any reason; he just refused to go. I was mortified and had to keep making excuses when they would ask again. Another time, when a couple who had been my friends before I met Dan visited, a few hours into the visit he stood up and announced he we was going to bed, said good night, and left the room. My friends were embarrassed and stated nervously, "Oh, we must have stayed too long." I was horrified. I tried to get them to remain but they made a swift exit. I was furious with him, but he didn't seem to see what the big deal was. So we spent much of our social time with his older brother and wife, with whom he was very close and seemed most comfortable.

After two and a half years of marriage, we attended Dan's maternal grandmother's funeral in New York. While I had been to several family members' funerals in my life, it was the first wake and funeral he had attended in his almost thirty years. He was miserable and restless all day, and rude to his family. He snapped at his mother and sisters, had an angry look on his face, and seemed distracted and agitated. After the service, he refused to go to his aunt's house for the repast. He insisted that we go directly home to New Jersey. I tried to persuade him to attend the repast for his mother's sake, but when he refused, I dutifully went home with him since I had no way to get back otherwise. Once again I was embarrassed and appalled and felt helpless to remedy the situation. I had no idea what was bothering him, and he would not confide anything to me. I had seen him angry and unhappy in the past, but this was at a level I had never witnessed, especially the way he was treating his family. When we got home, I announced that I was going to my parents' house for an hour or two. I needed to get away from him, his foul mood, and the day. I went to my mom's and had a cup of coffee. She was busy preparing dinner, and I sat quietly at her kitchen table, trying to absorb what had happened. I had been dealing with his antisocial behavior for some time and was at a loss as to what to make of it or how to deal with it.

I returned home a little over an hour later with nothing resolved in my mind. I found him sitting on the floor in our den with the classified ads section of the local newspaper spread out in front of him. Without looking up, he announced flatly, "I'm looking for apartments. I'm moving out. I don't want to be married anymore."

My whole being felt as if it were being plunged into an ice water bath. It took a few seconds for me to process what he had said. My mind repeated it a few times to be sure I'd heard right and to consider the implications. I couldn't even speak. Our marriage may not have been perfect, but it wasn't entirely unhappy either – at least not from my vantage point. We had our pleasant rituals, or so I thought, such as buying the Sunday *New York Times* on Saturday evening and working on the crossword puzzle together into the wee hours of the night, visiting flea markets and antique shops on weekends (when we were breaking up, he angrily proclaimed how much he hated going to those markets and stores, something he had never expressed in all our years together), and puttering around our old fixer-upper house. I had invested myself in the relationship and thought we could still make a go of it. In hindsight, I was delusional.

Not knowing what else to do, I encouraged him to call his older brother, Jake (not his real name) whose opinion and advice he had always relied on heavily. I thought he was just having a strong reaction to the funeral and loss. He made the call and came back into the room, relating that his brother said that "we" needed to see a marriage counselor. Here I thought that he was the one having the problem, and now all of a sudden it was "us." He seemed to have a new resolve, as if someone had given him an assignment with a deadline. His brother's wife even recommended a counselor that she knew. I always found Dan to be easily swayed by certain sources that he relied on, so if his brother told him we needed to see a marriage counselor then, by God, he was going to do it! I was happy to comply, hoping that at least it would buy some time for us to try to work things out. The thought of separating or getting divorced was a subject I didn't even consider. I still cared for him in spite of all the tribulations.

We agreed that we had some issues to work out and would commit to working on them. I remember us eventually kneeling on the floor that day, hugging each other and crying, admitting that our relationship was far from perfect and agreeing that we could make it better. It gave me some sense of hope.

Counseling did not go well. Outside of sessions, we bickered constantly. Although we'd had our arguments and disagreements previously, there would always be periods of calm between the battles. But the fighting was now escalating to a new level. There was no civility, only anger and hurt. As I look back, I realize that there were a lot of conflicts just under the surface that both of us had been denying, burying, or keeping from each other related to money, lack of physical intimacy, his not wanting to socialize, and so on. After only a few sessions, the therapist suggested we each see her separately, which we did.

Shortly after we started counseling, Dan began to go out occasionally with friends from work − at least that's what he told me. I was glad he was doing it because he rarely seemed to do anything for fun. I had encouraged him to socialize with his coworkers, but before this, he'd never seemed interested, preferring the solitude of home. So I was relieved and happy when he said he was going out after work. Things had gotten tense at home, and I thought it would be a good break for both of us.

Around this time, we'd been arguing about buying new speakers for our stereo system. I didn't think we needed them, but he really wanted them. In an effort to be accommodating, I finally agreed to go out and look at speakers with him one Friday evening. We made a date for six p.m., when we'd both be home from work. That night, six o'clock came and went. No husband and no phone call (this was in the days before cell phones). Finally nine p.m. rolled around, and he came sauntering in. I was livid. He walked past the door of the room I was sitting in, sat in a chair in the next room where I could see him, and again without looking at me he declared in a very bland tone, "I'm seeing someone else."

Right then, something inside of me changed. Any softness seemed to harden. Any lingering innocence evaporated. It was something I never saw coming. I've often heard so-called experts say that the signs of infidelity are always there. Later, our counselor even said to me, "You must have known." But I hadn't known. When you trust someone and love him, you don't read into everything that happens and look for double meanings.

After the first bombshell a few weeks earlier, when he said he didn't want to be married and was moving out, this one pushed me almost into a catatonic state. I didn't know how to respond. This scenario wasn't in my marriage playbook. I thought I should be angry but felt absolutely nothing. It was as if my ability to react was on lockdown. Feeling compelled to say or do something, I forced myself to start yelling things like, "I can't even look at you." Once I began to respond as I'd seen others do on TV or in movies, my real feelings started to emerge. I felt lost, alone, empty, beaten, broken, hollow, and worthless. I thought that I should leave the house rather than stay in the same space with him. So in soap opera fashion, I yelled that I was leaving. But where to go?

I called a girlfriend, but her line was busy. If she was on the phone, at least I knew she was home. I packed a bag and got into my car. I drove to her apartment about thirty minutes away. Fortunately, she was home and told me I could stay as long as I needed to. I was too embarrassed to call anyone in my family, so I called my husband's brother. Jake was a businessman who seemed worldly and intelligent and who, ironically, had left his own wife years earlier for another woman to whom he was currently married. He had always been friendly toward me, and while I can't say I was close to him or knew him well, we did have a comfortable familial relationship. So here I was on the phone, now sobbing uncontrollably, telling him what had happened as the reality of it all was still sinking in for me. I needed some advice myself this time. He told me I should contact a lawyer. I didn't know what I'd expected to hear from him, but I thought, A *lawyer*? *Really*? That sounded so final, so serious, and so scary. I wasn't ready for that step.

The next morning my friend suggested that we go to a local diner for breakfast. Eating was the last thing on my mind, but she told me, as good friends do, that I had to eat something. When the server placed a plate with two over-easy eggs and home fries in front of me, I took one look at it and felt an overpowering wave of nausea wrack my body. No food would pass my lips that day. (In fact, I hardly ate or slept over the next two weeks, losing fifteen pounds. I was shutting down physically and emotionally.)

After breakfast, I called my husband to see if we could meet at home later in the day to "talk." I guess, in my heart, I still wasn't ready to just let the whole thing go, even though I thought that was what usually happened when one person cheated on the other. He told me he couldn't meet with me because he had a date. Can you imagine? I was incredulous that he couldn't spare a few minutes for me and begged him to just talk to me for fifteen minutes before he went out. I have no idea what I hoped to accomplish, but I needed to be clear on a few things about this other woman and the status of our relationship. He finally agreed to speak briefly with me. When I got back to the house, he was all showered and shaved, in a pressed yellow shirt and cologne, ready for his rendezvous. He'd rarely paid that much attention to his appearance since we started dating. It made me feel like choking or vomiting.

I asked him if there was any way we could salvage our marriage, and he said there wasn't. He wanted to be with this other woman and that was that. I asked him some questions about her – questions that a woman who has been cheated on is desperate to know and yet is repulsed by the answers: Where had he met her? What did she look like? How long had he been seeing her? Did he love her? How was the sex? There was a hunger for details. He answered these questions reluctantly, rolling his eyes after each inquiry. He confessed that he met her at a bar while out with work friends one night, he'd been seeing her for several months, she was blonde and attractive, he did love her, and that the sex was "regular," whatever that meant. My nonexistent self-esteem fell to the subzero level.

Once he left for his "girlfriend's" house, I began to accept the fact that my marriage was over and that I was going to be single again. Needless to say, he didn't come home that night. The next day he called me at work, crying and telling me that he'd made a terrible mistake and that he wanted to come back home. Still hoping that there was even a slight chance of reconciliation, I agreed to meet with him. We decided that we would try one more time. Clearly it was not a well-thought-out decision on my part or his. But I was doing everything I could to avoid going to divorce court because of the shame, embarrassment, sense of failure, and probably even the fear of being alone again. I had flashes of myself as Hester Prynne from *The Scarlet Letter*. But instead of walking around with a giant "A" on my chest for Adultery as she was forced to do, I would be required to wear the letter

"D" for Divorced as the villagers mocked and jeered me.

After another week or two of living together, I received yet another call from him one evening before he had come home from work. He said he was at a local diner with his girlfriend and that he wasn't coming home anymore. "It's over," he proclaimed. I begged him to come home one last time to tell me this to my face and not over the telephone. He said he couldn't. I couldn't imagine how he must have felt about me to react that way. Was I so repulsive, repugnant, ugly, insensitive, ignorant, obnoxious, controlling, intolerant, or whatever? My self-regard was so low that I could only see my own perceived shortcomings in this situation. I didn't even consider that his own shame and self-doubts could be driving his actions.

It's interesting to note that Dan had always expressed a dread of turning thirty years old. Not surprisingly, all of this was occurring the year before his thirtieth birthday. Oh yes, and he was calling from a diner named Peter Pan. To this day when I see something with that name on it, my mind momentarily goes back to that night, one of the lowest points of my life.

I was distraught but had to face the reality that he "wasn't coming home anymore." Once again, I began to envision life on my own. My inner voice was reminding me that I had been on my own in the past and that I could do it again and that maybe it wouldn't even be so bad. At least I wouldn't have to pander to him, which did sound rather appealing. After another sleepless night, I went into work a little shaky but eager for the support of my coworkers, many of whom were also experiencing domestic strife. I hadn't been at my desk an hour when I received yet another "morning after" phone call. Incredulously, Dan repeated his teary confession and plea one more time, blubbering that he had made a terrible mistake and wanted to be with me and come home again.

This was the moment when I finally began to take control of my life back. I knew that if I didn't stand up for myself and simply allowed this craziness to continue, I would get sick, get addicted to something, or act out in some inappropriate way. And no other person is worth that. In the book *Lucky*, author Alice Sebold, who was brutally raped as a young woman, writes, "You have to save yourself or you remain unsaved."

This time I told *him* that it was over. I was simply fed up with Dan's manipulations, indecisiveness, and deceitfulness, not to mention the emotional ping pong he was playing with me. I began to see him for who he really was: a man who was lost, confused, hurting, disappointed in his own life, and angry, with many unresolved issues from his past. Perhaps I'd always known these things about him but naively thought I could help him in some way or that he would change. At the very least, I had opted to put blinders on through most of our relationship. The blinders were now off.

I told him I wanted him to move out of our home. He refused, stating that it was his house, too. Not knowing how to force him out, and because someone had told me that if I moved out I might forfeit certain rights, I decided to stay, and we spent a few miserable weeks under the same roof, sleeping in separate bedrooms and living separate lives. It was painful and insane, but I didn't know what else to do. There's no procedure manual for a marriage breaking up, and I hadn't yet contacted an attorney. The clincher was when I needed to talk to him about something while at home one evening, and he told me he was busy on the phone with his girlfriend. Finally, I told him that the arrangement was not working out. He agreed and said he would start looking for an apartment. He claimed to be searching the classified ads each day for a place, but said he wasn't finding anything he could afford. After a time, it was apparent that he was in no hurry to leave, and I would have to take matters into my own hands if he was ever going to get out.

Around that time, I became friendly with a woman I had met at the weight control center. She was renting a studio apartment nearby. She told me one day that she was tired of apartment life and wished she could find a house to share with someone. I got an idea! I told her about my home/marital situation and suggested that she might consider moving in with me and that perhaps my husband could move into her studio. She was excited at the prospect. I needed a roommate to help pay the mortgage, since I just knew Dan wouldn't contribute, and he needed some incentive to get the hell out of my space. I told him about it, we went to look at the studio, and he decided to take it. Mission accomplished!

Dan and I agreed to a no-fault divorce, which in New

Jersey required an eighteen-month legal separation. I found an attorney, we got a legal agreement, and our separation began. As the end of the separation got close, we put the house – the only thing of value that we jointly owned – on the market and sold it. I moved into a tiny apartment but was happy to be on my own again.

On the day of our official divorce decree, we had to show up at the courthouse in Newark, New Jersey. I asked my mother to go with me. I wore a beautiful white gauze outfit that day. I can't help reflecting on the irony of that. I think it was a symbol of my starting over. When my soon-to-be-ex saw me at the courthouse, he gave me a big smile and wave as if we were old friends who had just happened to bump into each other in divorce court. This after we had battled bitterly for weeks prior, with both of our lawyers present, over some brass andirons and a crockery tea set that had been wedding shower gifts, both of which he told me he didn't want at the last minute. It's amazing the things two divorcing spouses can find to argue over. I couldn't even look at him and just turned away. I was required to get into the witness box in the courtroom while the judge asked me if I was sure I wanted to get divorced and if I was sure I didn't want or need alimony. Thank God the judge didn't ask my ex the same question because I believe I was making more money than he was at that time. I said I was sure on all counts. And then it became official: I was an un-married woman once again. I was twenty-eight-years-old and relieved to be finally disconnected from Dan, not only physically, but now legally as well. I felt a sense of freedom.

Our divorce affected me in several different ways. For years, I felt like the scorned woman, the woman whose husband had "cheated on her." There is a certain stigma about being in that role; you feel as if people are whispering behind your back that you must have somehow driven the man into another woman's arms. Funny how some people always assume it was the jilted spouse's fault when things go awry. I remember meeting a guy in a club one evening, after I told him I was getting divorced, he said in all seriousness and with an air of surprise, "Gee, you don't *seem* like a bitch."

I projected a lot of anger toward my ex after our split and repeatedly asked myself, "How could he do this to me?" I focused on what I saw as the ultimate betrayal and perfected the victim persona, which is a great way to avoid taking any responsibility for your own life and heap all the blame on others. I even agonized over being the first in my immediate family (although not the last) to get a divorce. Needless to say, there was lots of drama going on in my head and my life – much of it self-created.

In her book *Calling All Women – From Competition to Connection*, author and family therapist Sharon Wegscheider-Cruse says, "There is no such thing as a wronged spouse. There are only marriages in which there is conflict and pain." In other words, breakups are usually not the fault of one person or the other, but simply the result of a "coupling" that doesn't work. Of course it is always nice to play the martyr and blame someone else for what went wrong in our lives. But the time comes when you have to stop telling your negative stories, those tales about how someone hurt you or did you wrong or the mistakes you made or the disadvantages you face, and cease using them as roadblocks to becoming a full person and being fully alive. It's not easy to give up the victim role and take responsibility for your own life and outcomes. But if you don't, you put someone else in charge of your life and your happiness.

When I began to awaken spiritually (more on that in chapter 5), after years of self-work and life experience, I came to realize that the entire relationship, including its demise, was simply – albeit painfully – part of my life's story. It was necessary to propel me forward on my own path. I often say I would not go back and change it because it is part of who I am. The universe seems to have a way of nudging us along our path in life. And, as you'll learn as you read on, it led me to meeting the love of my life.

While Dan and I we were still legally married, but had been separated for several months, I resigned from my job at the medical weight control center. I had no other job lined up and no other means of support. I knew I would eventually need to get another job, but I had to look for something that did not require the level of responsibility, focus, and time commitment that my current job required. I just wasn't emotionally capable of that anymore. It was a risky move, but I felt as though I had no choice. I did some cocktail waitressing at a friend's bar and had my roommate to help pay the mortgage and utilities. But there was a stretch when I periodically didn't have any food in the house and no extra money to buy some. I didn't have family nearby at that time (they had moved away) and I was too proud, and embarrassed, to ask for help. So I often went hungry. This experience taught me to remember that people who are going through challenging times – financial, emotional, physical, spiritual – always need help and support even if they say they don't or don't ask for help. It's hard for most of us to ask for help, even when we are destitute.

One day I saw a quote on a Kenny Rankin album cover that said something like, "When you've lost everything, you still have your dreams." Those words were like an emotional lifeline thrown to me at a time when I was adrift in a sea of hopelessness and despair. So during this time, while still unemployed (except for occasional waitressing), I reconnected with my music. I had done some singing accompanied by my acoustic guitar in high school and then in nursing school, mostly at the weddings of family and friends, a funeral, and the occasional party or local club date. I signed up for a group-singing course in New York City, at the now-defunct Guitar Learning Center started by Paul Simon. I had always toyed with doing more performing. In class, I met a woman who also sang and played guitar. She would become my second housemate (housemate number one was getting ready to relocate) and the other half of a duet. We both played twelve-string acoustic guitars and had voices that melded perfectly, creating harmony that sounded angelic to my ears and others'. So we decided to take our show on the road.

She and I started rehearsing incessantly and put together an eclectic montage of music including folk rock, blues, popular, and old folk songs. Someone referred to us as a female version of Simon and Garfunkel. We began playing local clubs and talked about taking it to the next level – looking for bigger and higher-paying gigs in New York and who knows where from there.

Unfortunately, our musical harmony did not translate into our friendship, and we found ourselves at odds over an increasing number of things. Maybe sharing living space and performing together was just too much. Perhaps our lives were starting to move in differing directions. Whatever it was, we knew our musical (and cohabitation) union was coming to an end.

Fortunately, we were still performing in a local club when a man came in one night and sat at the bar about twenty feet away from the stage. I spotted him in the dimly lit, smoke-hazed room and thought he was someone I had recently met at a party who'd said he was going to come to the club to hear me sing. So while we finished our set, I looked in his direction and coyly smiled, waved, and winked in a flirtatious manner. When the set was done, I walked in his direction. As I got closer, I realized – to my horror – that the man was not who I thought he was. In fact, he was a total stranger! This man – dark-haired and mustached like the one from the party – was looking directly at me now because it was obvious I was headed straight for him. My panic started to swell as the distance between us shrank. When I got right next to him, now knowing for sure that we had never met and embarrassed beyond words, I said to him, feeling that I had to say something at this point, "I don't know you, do I." I spoke it not as a question but as a statement of fact.

He looked rather dumbfounded and said blankly, "I don't think so." I turned on my heels and started to move away as fast as I could, mortified at my own actions. Then, realizing that I had been the one waving, smiling, and then approaching him, I decided to turn around and go back, extend my hand to shake, and introduce myself. He shook my hand but still had a rather blank, if not cautious, expression on his face. He told me his name was Joe. I got away as fast as I could and was relieved when it was time to start singing and strumming again. At some point during that set, he got up and left the club. *Phew!* I thought.

But I couldn't get this stranger out of my mind. He had a rugged good look about him – a Charles Bronson type. He was dressed clean and casual, in jeans and a blazer. He appeared to be about the same age as me. There was something about his deep brown eyes that seemed to reach out of his head and grab hold of my soul. The feeling was so powerful that it was frightening. When I told my sister, she warned me to stay away from him (if I ever saw him again) if anything at all about him was scary. But there was nothing ominous about this mild-mannered man; it was the intensity of my emotional reaction at being near him that was alarming, since I had never experienced anything like that before.

Joe came back to the club the next week when my partner and I were performing again. This time, he sat close to the stage. During a break I went up to him, ignoring my sister's admonition, and gave him a friendly, "Hi." After all, we were old friends now! As we talked, he told me he was divorced, and I remember replying glibly, "Join the club." We chatted for a while and then he asked me awkwardly if I "went out." I didn't know if he wanted to step outside for fresh air or what! I finally realized he was trying to ask me out and was apparently attempting to ascertain if I was available. I agreed to see him the next week.

By chance, our first date was on the Christian holy day Good Friday. Joe picked me up at my house and suggested that we go for a drink at a local pub and then into Times Square in New York City to walk around. It sounded like a fun and adventurous evening! Having been raised Catholic, I hoped God would forgive me for partying rather than going to church that day. Joe drove a late-model Fiat Spider sports car. It was a two-seater convertible and he had the top down on that balmy spring evening. It all added to the romanticism of the night, at least up until a point.

After our drink in a restaurant where, two years later, we would have our wedding reception, we headed into the big city. While on a dingy stretch of road in a seedy part of New Jersey just outside of Manhattan, the car suddenly began to sputter, and it died as Joe maneuvered to the shoulder. He quickly assured me that he could remedy the situation and requested that I sit in the driver's seat and "pop the clutch" (pressing down on the clutch pedal and then quickly releasing it when the car is in motion) while he got out and pushed the car from behind in an effort to start the engine. I gave it a shot but, having never attempted this before, I was nervous and unsure about how to do it in spite of Joe's instructions. Our efforts were not successful. Since the car was so small and lightweight and I am of sturdy eastern European stock (my ancestry is Polish), I suggested that Joe pop the clutch and I push. So there I was on our first date, fortuitously dressed casually and in flats, pushing my new boyfriend's car down the litter-strewn shoulder of a Jersey thoroughfare. Our reversal of roles worked well, and the Fiat's engine coughed back to life.

We decided that continuing into New York City was not the best idea under the circumstances, so Joe offered to prepare dinner for me, at his apartment, to make amends. Although it almost sounded like a ploy to get me alone, I have to admit I was intrigued by the offer of a homemade meal and was curious to witness his culinary talents. Using what he had on hand in his bachelor pad, he made me scrambled eggs and toast. I recall that he added champagne to the eggs – nice touch. He was obviously comfortable in the kitchen. *Hmm*, I considered, *a man who can cook.* This guy was getting more attractive by the minute. Fortunately the Fiat did start up later that evening and he was able to take me home. We agreed to go out again and began dating weekly.

Joe had apparently been dating quite a bit before meeting me, and I knew he was still seeing other women. So after a series of Friday night dates with him, when I assumed he had a "better" date on Saturday nights, I let him know I wasn't interested in playing second string. As deep as my feelings had already gotten for him, I was willing to stop seeing him if I wasn't a priority in his life. This was a new version of me, more resolute and confident than in previous relationships, bolstered by the experience of standing up for my own life and happiness in my first marriage. I was no longer willing to settle in love. I wanted more out of life and now felt that I deserved it. My confronting Joe with what I wanted and needed, and being willing to move along if I couldn't find it with him, was a turning point in our relationship. Joe told me that he didn't want to see anyone else going forward and then murmured, "I think I love you." I happily agreed to an exclusive relationship and told him, "I think I love you, too."

Joe had two children from his previous marriage, who were twelve and fourteen years old when I met him – a boy and a girl. My sister recalls that I once told her I would like to someday marry a man who already had children. Although I don't remember saying that or even thinking it, it must have been in my psyche. I always loved children (still do) but never had any desire to have any of my own. Joe didn't want to have any more children, so we were in sync in that regard. I'm now convinced that his children were meant to be in my life.

Our two-year courtship was challenging because of Joe's family life. He was still paying alimony and child support and had a contentious relationship with his ex-wife. There were visitation schedules to navigate, trips to court (over every little thing, it seemed), and the challenges of trying to raise children when the parents can barely speak to one another in a civil tone. There was often yelling, fighting, and arguing between them all, either in person or by phone. Joe and I did have our alone time together, and we tried to do as many things with the children as we could when they were with us.

I still had my own place and was often relieved to go home in the evening to the peace and quiet of my little apartment, leaving the three of them to settle their own differences (or not). After some days or evenings where there was considerable bickering and high emotions with his ex-wife and kids, I would sit quietly in my home, my refuge, reminding myself that I could walk away from all of this any time I chose – for good. But by now I knew that at his core, Joe was a good man. He was honest, ethical, loving, compassionate, passionate about life, adventurous, and fun-loving. I'd witnessed how he interacted with family and friends and even strangers and brought out the best in everyone, including me. Plus his sense of fun and humor were legendary. We had a lot of common interests, including camping and a love of the outdoors, music of all types, and travel. But Joe also had his own hobbies, including painting and fishing, which meant that he wasn't dependent on me to occupy his downtime, which I had sometimes thought that Dan was. Also important, Joe and I discussed issues related to money, family, and relationships while dating and found that we had similar values. This was a change from our first marriages, where both parties seemed to be in a constant tug-of-war with each other on these key matters. All of these wonderful characteristics and attributes far outweighed any challenges, present or future, that we might endure. He lifted me up in every way.

All of this was in stark contrast to my first marriage, where I felt I had to constantly placate my husband to keep the peace at home and then do damage control with friends and relatives when he was rude. Back then, I didn't have the sense of self-worth or the courage to honor my own needs, speak up for myself, and make a change if things were unsatisfactory. I felt that I had to work around whatever was at hand and try to make the best of it. This was because I viewed myself as a very imperfect woman and human being who had to take what she could get. But I was now making a very deliberate choice to be with Joe because of the person he was and how he made me feel, and not because being with him seemed like a convenient arrangement, which was what had pulled me to Dan years earlier.

When Joe and I first met, about six months after my legal separation started, the issue of marriage was off the table (and would be for another year) because I was still legally married to Dan. Joe had already been divorced for a few years. But shortly after my divorce did become final, while out to dinner in a casual restaurant one evening, Joe leaned across the table toward me and asked expectantly, with a big smile on his face, "So when are we getting married?" The question startled and frightened me. While I was absolutely in love with Joe and wanted to spend the rest of my life with him, I was scared to get married a second time because I never wanted to get divorced again. I told him I needed to think it over.

Of course there are no guarantees in life but both Joe and I had been through painful marriages and divorces and were clearer than ever about what worked in a relationship and what didn't, and what was important to each of us. Additionally, because of our past heartaches, hardships, and disappointments we had both come into this relationship as stronger, more whole, and more confident human beings. In spite of my fears about remarriage in general, I sensed deep down that it was the right thing to do and I eventually consented. I was willing to take a chance on Joe, his kids, and our relationship. I have never regretted my choice to marry Joe and often tell others that it is best decision I ever made in my life.

This time we did it right. We met with the pastor of a Methodist church in our community, who agreed to marry us. Joe and I were both raised Catholic but were not practicing and probably weren't eligible to be married in a Catholic church anyway since we were both divorced. I bought a beautiful off-white, tea-length wedding dress in a bridal shop. We only had immediate family present since it was a second wedding and we wanted to keep it small. We had an elegant dinner in an old train car that was part of the restaurant where Joe and I had out first date. We exchanged rings and went on a magical and romantic honeymoon to Quebec, Canada. I had indeed finally met, and married, the love of my life, and was willing to work as hard as necessary to make this relationship happy and strong.

Upon returning from our honeymoon, I transitioned into the role of stepparent to two teenagers, which was both fun and challenging. I had a hard time initially figuring out how I fit into their lives. But all of us, the kids included, were feeling our way through this new normal and trying our best to work things out. I was twenty-nine-years-old when I married Joe, and the kids were then fourteen and sixteen. Although this may seem like a relatively small age difference, the kids and I were very clearly of two different generations. Joe and I, although eleven years apart in age, always seemed at a similar stage of life to one another. I took on a parental role without attempting to replace their own mother. So the age differences were never an issue in our relationships.

Today we have a close, loving family unit. All four of us enjoy each other's company, live within an hour of each other, and know that we have each other's backs at all times. For all the trials and tribulations of the coming together of this new family, it was worth the struggle to get to where we are today. My family has now grown to include another daughter (our son's wife) and two grandsons — one that our son and "second daughter" had together, and one that this daughter had from a previous marriage. Somehow it was all meant to be. God bless every step of that broken road that made us, and keeps us, a family.

In reflecting, I had several relationships with men prior to meeting Joe, including my first marriage, none of which were particularly satisfying or nurturing. Most of those men disappointed me in many ways, broke my heart, let me down, cheated on me, and otherwise made me feel like I was less than I am. Were they to blame for my heartache and misery? Although they did play a part, I can now say that I was an active participant, or enabler, in the dysfunction of the relationship by tolerating or excusing bad behavior and by pushing my own happiness aside.

Confronting one's own unhappiness (not to mention confronting another person's, as with my first husband), especially if it means making changes, is scary. We often find unhealthy ways to work around the unhappiness, such as lowering our expectations of what a relationship should be or could be, or convincing ourselves that what we want isn't out there or is unrealistic, or that we don't deserve something better. We do this with jobs, careers, relationships, and our own dreams. We stay in an unhappy or mediocre comfort zone rather than risk becoming happy by pursuing something that is unknown or uncertain. Many of us exist in that self-imposed prison, serving a sentence for a crime we never committed.

Staying in a bad or unsatisfying situation is unhealthy. It takes a toll on you physically, emotionally, and spiritually. It erodes your self-esteem, and if you stay long enough without resolution, the damage can be irreparable. It can lead to depression, physical illness, addiction, and acting out in inappropriate ways. Sometimes letting go of what is familiar, even when it feels dangerous to do so, is the best way to protect our physical and emotional health.

I have known many women over the years who have never gotten over the breakup of a significant relationship when their partner is the one who opts out, either through having an affair, physical or emotional cruelty, or just leaving. I have witnessed with sadness how they let that one relationship and its outcome define them and direct the rest of their lives. They continue to believe that if they could just get thinner or prettier or better in bed they could eventually win him back. Rather than coming to the understanding that their ex has issues of his own to resolve or that the pair of them are simply incompatible, these women believe the breakup is validation of their own inferiority and failure as women and wives. But as mythologist Joseph Campbell said, "We must be willing to let go of the life we planned so as to have the life that is waiting for us." In other words, it's only when we let go of what doesn't work for us or bring us joy and happiness, whether a relationship, a behavior pattern, or a thought process, that we allow who and what we want to find us.

LESSONS LEARNED

---

1. Life may not turn out as you planned, but there is always another life waiting for you as long as you don't let the old one destroy you or hold you back.

2. Staying in a bad or unsatisfying situation is not physically, emotionally, or spiritually healthy. It erodes your self-esteem, and the damage can be irreparable.

3. Playing the victim puts someone else in charge of your life and happiness.

4. Telling your negative stories serves as a roadblock to living a full life and becoming a full person. Create a new, positive story.

5. When you've lost everything, you still have your dreams.

6. People who are going through challenging times always need help and support, even if they say they don't or don't ask for help.

7. Family isn't always a result of biology.

RECOMMENDED READING

Richardson, Cheryl. *Stand Up For Your Life: A Practical Step-By-Step Plan to Build Inner Confidence and Personal Power*. New York: Free Press, 2003.

Sebold, Alice. *Lucky: a Memoir*. New York: Scribner, 1999.

Wegscheider-Cruse, Sharon. *Calling All Women — From Competition to Connection: Advice and Inspiration for Women of All Ages*. Deerfield Beach, FL: Health Communications, 2009.

chapter three

CARING FOR MY MOST
IMPORTANT ASSET — ME

Don't sacrifice yourself too much, because if you
sacrifice too much, there's nothing else you can give
and nobody will care for you.

—KARL LAGERFELD

JOE STARTED SELLING REAL ESTATE ABOUT A YEAR BEFORE
his MS diagnosis. Prior to this, he had left the corporate
world, where he had worked throughout his thirty-year
career, after his company moved out of state. He had no
interest in moving with them and was looking for a
different lifestyle, so we jointly agreed to the change.
This was a big decision for us because with me planning
to start a business, we would both be self-employed with
no corporate benefits, a rather risky proposition.

Joe loved real estate, and was a natural salesman and
a genuine people person. I often said that he could talk
to anyone about almost any subject and that everyone

who met him liked him. But two years after his diagnosis, and one year after I did start the business, he was struggling to climb stairs, getting exhausted easily, and walking more laboriously, all making it increasingly difficult for him to do his job. One of those defining moments eventually occurred – those times when truth smacks you hard across the face to get your attention. Joe, who had progressed to using a cane for support, fell while trying to pull an "Open House" sign out of the ground. The ground was wet and soft from a prior rain, and he lost his balance. He wasn't able to get right back up because of his MS and there he lay, in a business suit and tie, rolling around on someone's prize lawn. The house was on a busy street and from his ground-level vantage point he could see cars whizzing by and people glancing at him. He imagined that the passersby assumed he was drunk. He eventually was able to get on his hands and knees and push himself up, but felt embarrassed and defeated.

After that incident, we knew we had to face a heartbreaking reality: Joe was no longer able to work. Along with that came another new reality. I would become the primary financial support of our family. Joe was now fifty-four, and I was forty-three. Our kids were grown and out of the house, but there were mortgage and car payments, health insurance premiums, and all the miscellaneous expenses of daily life. To say I was scared and overwhelmed would be an understatement. My speaking business was still young, and I was struggling to build it. My cash flow fluctuated wildly, and I was investing any meager profits I did make back into the business. Sometimes I had successes, but there were often lulls between them. I wasn't sure I could earn enough to carry our expenses alone.

Fear can be paralyzing, but in this case it worked as a great motivator. The realization that we might not eat or be able to pay our bills unless I brought in sufficient money with my business energized me. There is nothing better to light a fire under you than being responsible for putting food on the table for your family and keeping a roof over their heads. I recommitted myself to building the business with a new focus, drive, and determination that I knew would be needed to make it work.

We also immediately looked over our expenses and found ways to cut back on our cost of living. I began planning budget menus ahead of time, shopping the food sales, and preparing all our meals at home – we stopped eating out or ordering in. We cut our entertainment expenses, such as movies at the theater, and made do with what we had in terms of clothes and accessories. I even found less-expensive ways to clean the house, such as using vinegar and water in place of those fancy sprays and wipes. Where I was previously at leisure to spend money on almost anything I wanted, within reason – a magazine, a new hair product, a book, a candy bar – I now had to consider every purchase, even one for fifty cents. I had a finite amount of cash in my wallet and had to make it last. If I didn't absolutely need something, I didn't buy it. The word "frugal" took on a whole new meaning in our lives. I often hear people who make good salaries declare, "I couldn't possibly live on less than I'm making now." Yet it is absolutely amazing how little you can live on when you put your mind to it.

Even though we cut our expenditures substantially, I still had to ramp up my business to provide a higher and more sustained income for us to survive financially. In an effort to inject energy and strength into my business, I became aggressive in the pursuit of personal and professional development. There was so much learning and growing to do. Living outside of my comfort zone became a way of life. Over the next several years I enrolled in graduate school, got active in − and eventually became president of − a 140-member women's business association, and wrote my first book. There was a sense of urgency to make things happen. As a result of all of this, plus endless hours making sales and networking phone calls, developing new material for presentations, and building professional relationships, opportunities were coming my way and my business, including my income, grew. At the same time, I was doing virtually nothing to take care of myself or replenish the extraordinary amount of energy I was expending. This would eventually catch up with me.

We were still living in a two-story house when Joe began selling real estate. But after a few years, with Joe's increasing difficulty navigating the stairs to our bedroom, it became apparent that we would have to move into a ranch-style house with everything on one floor. So we went about the demanding ritual of preparing our current home for sale while looking for someplace new to live. Since I had a home-based office, I'd be moving my home *and* office. By this time, Joe wasn't able to do much physically, and he was emotionally overwhelmed by the move. He found it hard to make decisions about what he would keep and what he would get rid of, procrastinated packing his things, and spent a lot of time online playing solitaire, his favorite avoidance activity of the time. We had friends and family to help, but most of the onus was on me to make our relocation happen.

To save Joe's physical energy, I did all the initial house hunting with our realtor, and would then go back with Joe when I found something promising. I also had to do most of the packing of and sorting through our belongings. We had accumulated so much in our house. Once we found a home to buy, I had to find and hire a moving company, take care of the inspection, and get minor things fixed in our old house without much input or help from Joe. Plus I had to manage his growing anxiety over the move and all my other caregiver duties while keeping my business going.

We both loved old homes that had a lot of character and old-world craftsmanship. But most houses built prior to the 1950s were two stories, so we had to settle for something a little more contemporary, making the purchase decision even harder. We finally found a lovely one-story home built in 1953, with some nice features, including a wood-burning fireplace, hardwood floors, and built-in corner cabinets in the dining room. It was in Wall Township, the same town we were already living in. We were able to negotiate a purchase price that was almost exactly the same as what we got for the old house, keeping our overall expenses at the same level. (We did eventually have to make modifications to the new house, including ramps, an accessible bathroom, and wider doorways when Joe later started using a wheelchair.)

After we physically settled into our new house, it all came crashing down on me. I woke up one morning and realized that my interest in – and passion for – my business was gone. I had no more energy for it and didn't want to continue with it. This terrified me. I didn't want all I had accomplished in starting and building my business to slip away. I recall that I also momentarily considered hopping on a plane to Bali and leaving everyone and everything behind with no forwarding address. But after I rejected the notion of leaving the country, it suddenly became clear to me that if things continued on as they had been, I would get sick – or worse. When I stopped to analyze what was happening to me, I realized that my stress level had reached critical mass. For the last ten years or so, I had been totally focused on my family, my business, and my clients. And while I had invested in myself intellectually through college, self-study, and other pursuits, I had done virtually nothing to nourish my emotional, physical, or spiritual health. In other words, I had been expending large amounts of energy but was doing nothing to replenish that energy. The well was dry. I had nothing left to give.

As a nurse, I was acutely aware that chronically un-managed stress causes illness and even premature death. Fortunately, I had the presence of mind to consider my options: I could let it all slip away – which was horrible and unthinkable – or wake up to the fact that I had to give some priority to my own well-being and not just to that of my family, clients, and business. Once again, I used fear as a springboard to dive into action. It alerted me to the fact that something had to change. I needed to create some balance in my life before permanently burn-ing myself out.

Our financial situation had improved, thanks to my growing business, so I decided to join a lovely fitness club near our new home – but not for the reasons you might think. My friend Cathe, a fellow woman business owner and now a neighbor invited me to be her guest one day at this club where she was a member. And while it had a well-equipped gym and yoga classes and all that, what really sold me on joining myself was the private whirlpool and sauna in the ladies' locker room. I thought, *Wow, I don't have to wait until staying at a hotel with a whirlpool to enjoy one. Now I can go any time I want!*

I always felt guilty doing anything for myself, but "going to the gym" felt a little less indulgent, regardless of what I actually did there. So, getting into my workout clothes and picking up my gym bag, I'd head out of the house, announcing that I was going to "the club." But once there, my only activities might be soaking in the hot tub or floating on my back in the pool with my ears just under the surface of the water, where no one could talk to me, reach me by cell phone, or otherwise bother me. When I was alone, I was not required to think or act. The warm water surrounded me like a security blanket, making my body – and my troubles – seem temporarily weightless. It offered a much-needed respite. Even when I wasn't there, I felt better knowing that the gym was a just a short drive away.

I eventually started attending some of the fitness classes in addition to regular Jacuzzi time. Thanks to these activities, I began to feel a bit calmer and was able to renew enough interest in my business to carry on. Now that I was indoctrinated into the world of self-nurturing, or what is commonly referred to as self-care, I considered what else might be available to reduce my stress level and boost my energy. I had long wanted to get a massage, but I felt creepy thinking about getting mostly naked in a small room with a stranger! But when the salon where I was getting my hair cut hired a diminutive, soft-spoken massage therapist who seemed very friendly and nurturing, I felt safe enough to give it a shot. After my first session, which included a combination of low lighting, soft background music, lovely aromas, a heated treatment table, and the healing hands – not to mention soothing voice – of the therapist, I was hooked. The massage left me more relaxed than I had been in years. My muscles felt looser, my nerves were calmer, and my mind seemed to slow down, even if just for a while. It made such a difference that I began trying to go as often as possible. Whenever I started to feel a mounting sense of anxiety, that jangled feeling of disharmony, I knew it was time to make another appointment. Although the amount of stress in my life had not diminished, these stress-relief practices were making it easier to bear. I was gradually feeling more like myself – enthusiastic, energetic, and focused. I was coming to the realization that I was my most important asset and, as such, I had to invest in my own well-being with the same commitment and intensity that I did everything else in life.

Sometimes, when I am talking to others about self-care, they are quick to reply with something like, "Oh sure, as soon as I win the lottery!" implying that it costs a lot of money to get a massage or even join a gym. But as with everything else in life, there is more than one way to make things happen. Many massage clubs and day spas sell packages of treatments that you can buy in advance, which brings the cost down quite a bit. And massage schools usually offer nominally priced treatments by students who have already had considerable experience working on each other. I advise others to ask friends and family members for gift certificates to spas, wellness centers, salons, and gyms for birthdays, anniversaries, and special holidays. Some health insurance plans, and even some employers, cover the cost of joining a gym. But money isn't always the issue, although it is a convenient excuse. My newspaper horoscope once cautioned me not to be someone who knows the price of everything but the value of nothing.

Of course self-care doesn't have to cost any money at all. It encompasses anything that nurtures your body, mind, and spirit. It might include making time to journal or create art, take a walk, meet friends for coffee, or just sit quietly in a park or house of worship.

Perhaps the real issue is that many of us don't see our own self-care as important, so we don't make it a priority. People often say that women and caregivers put themselves at the bottom of their own to-do lists. In truth, we're usually not even on the list. And yet multiple sources verify that caregivers have higher mortality and other negative health outcomes than non-caregivers because of higher stress levels and lack of self-care. Whether you are a caregiver or not, the bottom line is that unmanaged stress will take a heavy toll.

We hear messages of "Take care of yourself," or, "Tend to your own self-care." But most of us pay that advice lip service. I used to think, "Yeah, yeah, I know I should. One of these days . . . when I get around to it." One of the most commonly used excuses is, "When I have time." I saw a poster that said, "'I don't have time' is the adult version of 'The dog ate my homework.'" Many of us make excuses rather than making commitments. When you come right down to it, we all find the time – and the money, for that matter – for those things that are truly important to us.

As I began to avail myself of various forms of self-nurturing, I became increasingly interested in learning more about how I could maximize my overall well-being. There's a popular expression that says, "When the student is ready, the teacher will appear." In other words, when we open ourselves up to new learning or are ready to change, the message, the opportunity, or the resource will make itself known. In some cases, we are probably just more willing to see something or someone that was available to us all along. But in other cases, I have come to realize, someone crosses our path at just the right moment and unwittingly has a message to deliver, either directly or indirectly. I refer to these people as "light sources" sent to help illuminate our path, to push us further along in our journey. One way to envision them would be as footlights (or in some cases spotlights) on the bigger stage of our life.

One such light source in my life was a woman named Lori, who was a nurse, personal trainer, and stand-up comic. Lori had originally attended one of my career seminars for nurses. She then sought me out for business coaching when she was in the process of launching a speaking and health-coaching business. She was about fifteen years younger than me and lived in a nearby town. We stayed in touch by email and phone after our initial meetings and eventually became friends. I was also an informal mentor to her. Lori was attractive and fit, a former competitive body builder and one-time contestant in the Mrs. New Jersey Pageant. She would use me as a "trial" subject when she was launching a new dietary or exercise regimen. I would try the program and give her feedback, which would help her refine her offerings to her clients.

During one of these trials, a year or so after I had started at the gym, Lori recommended I read the book *The Power of Full Engagement.* In it, authors Jim Loehr and Tony Schwartz describe why it is important to manage energy rather than time. They state, "Many of us treat life as a marathon that doesn't end until it finally ends for good." We've gotten so caught up in a cycle of "doing" – working at a constantly frantic pace in everyday life – that we have lost our sense of "being." They stress how vital it is to periodically disengage from life and work, or "shift from achievement to restoration," so that we can more passionately and fully reengage in life and work.

Loehr and Schwartz describe disengagement as a temporary pulling away – whether for a few moments or for a week or more – to shift gears, have a change of scenery, or refocus your thoughts and energies. Some short and sweet ways to disengage even for a few moments would be to step outside and enjoy nature, stretch, or close your eyes and take some deep breaths. Longer periods of disengagement might include hitting the gym, visiting a friend or neighbor, going on vacation, or taking a sabbatical from work. Disengagement and restoration allow us to function at our highest level physically and mentally. We're able to not only get more done but to fully focus, concentrate, be creative, be able to make decisions, be happy, and be healthy. This book solidified for me that just as I had to tend to my speaking business, I also had to tend to the "business" of self-care.

During the same time I'd been working with Lori, I got closer to a woman named Linda, whom I had met years earlier through the National Association of Women Business Owners (NAWBO). Linda was another light source in my life, who wound up inadvertently helping me along my own self-nurturing and spiritual development path. She was a few years older than me, also had an interest in antiques, and lived only a few towns away. We had known each other casually for many years, having jointly sat on the board of directors of the organization. Initially, we would see each other primarily at association functions and occasionally at an area antiques show. Linda had invited me to be a board member when she became president of the local chapter of NAWBO and later encouraged me to run for president to follow her, which I did and was successful. So I had always looked at her as a mentor of sorts. But we became closer after her husband Mike died, suddenly and unexpectedly, from pancreatic cancer about a year after I moved into my new house and joined the gym.

Prior to his diagnosis, Linda's husband had retired, and she was in the process of selling her bookkeeping business. Linda and Mike had looked forward to traveling and further pursuing one of the things they loved, buying and selling antiques. They'd anticipated spending even more time together. They had lovingly and painstakingly restored their historic home – a twenty-year project at long last completed. But her world had now been turned upside down, and the slate that outlined her future had also been wiped clean.

I was speaking in Australia when Mike died and felt terrible that I couldn't go to the wake and funeral and otherwise be there for Linda. So upon my return to the States, I asked her if we could meet for lunch. I hadn't even known Mike was sick prior to his death and wanted to hear what had happened plus lend support. We talked and cried over lunch as she related her harrowing tale of Mike falling sick and his subsequent rapid demise. We made a soul connection that day over Caesar salads. After our lunch, I began inviting Linda over for dinner regularly. We'd catch a movie when we could, and she would join Joe and me on some leisure outings, such as going to museums.

Even though my husband was alive, albeit becoming progressively more disabled each year, Linda and I now had an even closer bond based on loss, sadness, fear, and a forced "starting over." We were both strong, accomplished women who had plenty of baggage from previous relationships and life in general. We had worked hard (and are still working hard, but that's our little secret) to overcome feelings of inadequacy, inferiority, and all the other human frailties you can think of. There is comfort in talking to and spending time with others who share your challenges – no matter how devastating those challenges are. There is a quiet compassion and unspoken understanding of a shared experience. We occasionally cried together, shared our fears, supported and encouraged one another, and celebrated each other's milestones and accomplishments. There's a beautiful quote by Bernard Meltzer that goes, "A friend is someone who knows the song in your heart and can sing it back to you when you have forgotten the words." This quote helps to describe how Linda and I took turns lifting each other up over the years and underscores the value of true friendship.

Girlfriends and girl time are important. Yet when life gets busy and hectic, it's often our time with friends that suffers the most. However, there is plenty of research, including the famed Nurses' Health Study launched by Harvard University in 1975, to support that good friendships, especially for women, are linked to good health, more vitality as we age, and possibly even longer life, not to mention more joy. So nurturing those relationships and investing in them on an ongoing basis is vital to our health and happiness, and maintaining active friendships can be considered an important aspect of self-care.

While our friendship was burgeoning, Linda was having a difficult time dealing with her husband's death. In spite of urging from many people, she did not seek counseling or other support services to help her get through. She was trying to tough it out on her own, as I had so often tried to do myself, believing it was the "stronger" thing to do. She was in a state of profound grief, sadness, and mounting stress. I had been trying to get her to have a massage for a while, something she had never experienced. She always flatly rejected the notion, affirming that it was not for her. No matter how hard or how often I tried, she refused.

I'm not sure where the notion of toughing things out as a sign of strength comes from, but I now know that seeking help and support in times of struggle – whether from friends, family, or professionals – is actually the stronger and more practical thing to do. It takes courage to stand up and say, "I need help." And that very declaration, whether through the process of reaching out to someone or simply accepting help when it's offered, opens the door to healing.

After reading an article about how massage treatments are therapeutic for those who have lost a spouse or partner, I decided to take matters into my own hands, as good friends will often do when they see a friend suffering. I made two concurrent massage appointments for a day I knew Linda was available and told her in no uncertain terms that we were going together.

Sensing my determination (a nice way of saying I strong-armed her . . . in a good way), she nervously asked me what she should wear. I told her it didn't matter because she'd have to take off her clothes when we got there. Her next question: "Should I wear makeup?"

"No," I advised, "because sometimes they massage your face."

"I don't want anyone touching my face," she asserted, with a tinge of panic in her voice.

"Oh-kaaay," I cooed to calm her. "Just tell the therapist you don't want him or her to do that."

So we went to the day spa, and of course she wore full makeup because she never leaves the house without it. When I came out from my treatment, Linda was already finished. She was sitting on a bench, propped up against the wall like you would prop up an infant who doesn't yet have the muscle strength to sit without support. She had smudged mascara around her eyes and running down one cheek, disheveled hair, and a glassy look in her eyes. Her gaze very slowly made its way up to mine, and she said in a soft, almost slurred tone, "Woooooooow." When she was able to form a complete sentence, she added that the therapist said she was so "tight" that she would need at least two more treatments before she'd have some sense of physical equilibrium back. *Only two?* I thought.

After I dragged Linda to the spa that first time, she quickly became a self-care convert. I joke that I couldn't get her *out* of the spa after that, so I nicknamed her "Spa Girl." Massage, facials, waxings – you name it, and she got it done regularly. She also joined my gym and started to take regular exercise classes. All of this helped her keep her stress level under control, stay healthy and fit, make new friends, and start to create a new life for herself. Linda made self-care a priority, even though she came to it kicking and screaming.

This reconnection with Linda occurred during the year of my fiftieth birthday. Since starting at the gym about a year prior, and beginning to pay attention to my self-care needs, I had become able to manage my stress better. Although I still felt very tense at times, I had improved coping skills. Fortunately, my enthusiasm for my business had returned, and the business was doing well. We were now financially stable, if not comfortable. The new house was working out well for both of us. It was easier to maintain, and Joe was able to maneuver around well with his walker. However, I still had deep pain and sadness just under the surface that I was learning to work around, related to Joe's advancing illness. I could very easily be brought to tears if I started taking about his condition, so I mostly kept that to myself.

In spite of my underlying sorrow, and unlike the crisis I had experienced at age forty, fifty seemed like a cause to celebrate. It felt akin to reaching the summit of a tall mountain after a long, hard climb. But rather than planning for my descent, as one would after reaching a mountaintop, I realized that I could see farther than before and that there were even taller mountains to scale and so much left in the world to see and do.

I wanted to do something special for my fiftieth birthday, something I'd never done before, something big and worthy of the occasion, just to rejoice in my own life. After all, having been on the planet for half a century is quite an accomplishment, and worthy of a mid-centennial celebration! Birthday celebrations, I've come to realize, whether done alone or with friends and family, give us an opportunity to step back from the craziness of everyday life and reflect on where we are, how far we've already come, and where we might still want to go. They are a chance to honor ourselves, be good to ourselves, and enjoy ourselves, and I wanted to do just that.

I considered going to one of those destination spas where you walk around in a bathrobe all week, sipping smoothies and being pampered. My birthday is in December, and I live on the East Coast, so a warm climate and change of scenery would be perfect. I mentioned this desire to some friends and business colleagues and asked if anyone could recommend a good spa.

Lisa, a professional acquaintance, told me with great awe and enthusiasm about Miraval Resort and Spa in Arizona, a place she had visited on more than one occasion. She said that the place was beautiful, spiritual, magical, and incredibly relaxing. Lisa waxed poetic about the scrumptious food, beautiful desert setting, and several of the treatments she enjoyed, including "aqua Zen," where a therapist slowly moves your floating body around in a warm, shallow pool. She especially gushed about one of their signature programs, the Equine Experience, where you work with horses to get more in touch with yourself and your relationships.

I checked the place out online, and it seemed a bit pricey at first glance. Knowing that Lisa was a hardworking gal likely making a modest salary, and not what one would call well off, I figured that if she was spending her hard-earned money on the place, it must be worth it. But then, like many other things in my life, I put the spa in the back of my mind and went about my daily existence. Thinking about something and taking action to make it happen are two entirely different things.

I mentioned the idea to Linda and told her about the

resort Lisa had mentioned. Spa Girl got all excited and said, "Let's go! Get out your calendar, and let's pick a date!" Linda was financially solid, so the money was not an issue for her. Plus she was retired and had no one at home who she was responsible for. I wanted to go but was dragging my feet about making the commitment – of both time and money. I fretted that I'd be leaving my disabled husband behind for almost a week. Keep in mind that he was perfectly capable of taking care of himself at this point and was left alone regularly when I went on business trips. He was also supportive of my wanting to do this for myself, wonderful man that he is. But to think about leaving him for a pleasure trip – the guilt was overwhelming. It would also be the first time in my married life that I had considered taking a vacation without him.

You may be wondering why I didn't consider going with my husband rather than by myself or with a friend. For starters, Joe had no interest in flying (the desired destination was too far to drive), and it would have created a hardship for both of us anyway because of his disability. He also had no desire at that time to go to a spa – it was not his thing, or at least so it seemed to him without knowing more about the place. Additionally, I really felt that I needed some time to focus on myself for a change and take a break from my caregiver role. I knew that many women take girlfriend vacations, but it had never occurred to me to consider such a thing before.

It would have been easy for me to keep thinking

about going to the resort and talking about it but never acting on the desire if not for Spa Girl. Now she was pulling me along as I had done with her earlier when dragging her for her first massage. Like a dog with a bone, she wouldn't let go of the idea. She was incessant in her requests to have me get out my calendar and set a date for us to go to the resort together. With Linda's insistence and my husband's blessing, we finally went in February of 2004. We decided to go for only four nights on this first trip just in case we didn't love it. I was also trying to minimize my expenses for the trip, still feeling guilty about spending so much money on myself!

After flying into Tucson International Airport and spending the night at an airport hotel, we were transported to our destination by resort shuttle early the next morning. When we finally arrived at Miraval, with the Catalina Mountains as a backdrop, the plush greenery, the beautiful earth tones of the structures and interiors, and the bunnies and birds frolicking and flitting everywhere, I couldn't help but have a sense of awe and peace. The entire resort, including the guest rooms, had soothing Southwestern and Native American décor. There was sculpture and paintings all around, both inside and out, to further soothe and feed the senses. The food was healthy and light, yet decadent and plentiful at the same time. But most memorable was the wonderful aroma throughout, perhaps incense or candles or the fresh scent of nature, which calmed me down almost immediately. The entire place was like an oasis in the surrounding desert. Little did I realize that it would also be an oasis in both Linda's life and mine.

Most people think, as I did, that at these spas everyone spends time lying on chaise lounges with cucumber slices on their eyes and lazes around all week being indulgent, getting massages, facials, and the like. And while I'm sure some people may actually do just that, I soon realized that the "spa" portion of this resort was only a small part of what it had to offer me. In addition to the tranquil surroundings and beautiful facilities, there were classes and activities of all sorts for those who chose to partake of them.

The first workshop I attended, on the day we arrived, was on stress management. That shows you where my priorities were! There, I was introduced to the concept of mindfulness – something I had never heard of. Mindfulness, a basic tenet of Miraval, is the art of being truly alive and fully present in daily life. Most of us are usually ruminating about the past, projecting into (or worrying about) the future, or multitasking to the point that we're not fully focused on anything or anyone. As a result, we miss the full experience of everyday life, and our existence is unsatisfying and stressful.

As the week progressed, I felt myself beginning to relax and let go. Without the distractions of home, business, and everyday responsibilities, introspection and getting reacquainted with myself became my focus. Interestingly, on my third day at the spa, a woman who had shared the van ride with us from the airport to the spa spotted me and noted with astonishment that my face looked entirely different than it had when she initially met me. I was taken aback! Had my previous high stress level been that apparent and evident on my face? It was quite a wake-up call for me to realize not only how much I needed to "let go," but how visible my stress level was to the world (I'm sure in many ways other than my appearance).

Miraval also offered a journaling workshop because, as it was explained to me, writing is a way to learn more about yourself, clarify thoughts and feelings, and even uncover some buried emotions. It can also be a means of "releasing" hurtful and negative thoughts and memories. It is both a creative and a therapeutic process. I had recently started journaling at home, so I decided to attend the class.

Even though I was in a better place emotionally when I arrived at Miraval than I had been over a year earlier when we moved into the new house, I still carried a deep sense of sadness about Joe's illness, which had at that point been present in our lives for almost ten years. And while some things had eased up in terms of managing our home, my business, and Joe's condition, I still had intermittent periods of feeling completely overwhelmed by my life and sensing that I was losing control. While writing this book I found a piece I wrote during a journaling workshop on that first visit to Miraval. It illustrates my state of mind at the time (and other times):

I'm swimming in a sea of emotions and one by one they float to the surface – scary thoughts and feelings, fear, sadness, loss, and longing. I try to push them down. They are too painful. Trying so hard to hold it together. Feel like I'm drowning. What if I can't reach land? What if I'm too exhausted to swim to the shore? The undertow keeps pulling me out, dragging me to the bottom.

During those four days, I ate healthy gourmet food, swam, walked in the desert, had a few massages, and took daily meditation and yoga classes. I attended classes at my leisure given by nutritionists, psychologists, life coaches, exercise physiologists, and other specialists. I also spent quiet alone time just "being." My favorite spot to do the latter was at the "Bird Ramada," an area set up with benches under a trellis overlooking the spectacular mountains and surrounded by a collection of birdfeeders. If you sat still there for a few moments, partridges, hummingbirds, desert wrens, cardinals, and roadrunners would gather almost within touching distance. The sky, the mountains, the desert, the birds . . . I felt at one with the landscape and had a deep sense of peace.

At my urging, Linda attended a workshop titled "Grief, Loss, and Letting Go." It allowed her to better understand and cope with her loss and create a plan for moving forward with her life. She also went horseback riding in the desert and focused on fitness activities. She even got her hair styled and re-colored from white-blonde, which

I always thought was gray, to her original brunette. She looked, and felt, like a new woman.

Toward the end of our first stay at Miraval, Linda and I sat at an outdoor table sipping cups of tea and reflecting on the week's experience. We came to the conclusion that this excursion was not a luxury for us but rather a necessity – a necessity for our physical, emotional, and spiritual health and well-being. So Spa Girl and I vowed, at that moment, that we would return to Miraval each year together.

The value of making that joint commitment is that we held each other to it and enjoyed planning our trip each year and talking about past visits, reliving the experience over and over again – sometimes ad nauseam – to others in our lives. We did return to Miraval together for the next six years until Linda had some health issues to deal with and subsequently moved to Florida. I continue to return each year by myself or with other friends and family.

Wanting to share my experiences at Miraval and determined to find (create) a "reason" to go more than once a year, I also began holding workshops and retreats there for nurses and for women. It's interesting to note that after originally feeling apathetic toward my business and later feeling guilty about taking time away from that very business and my husband to focus on myself for that first resort visit, I learned a great lesson: taking time to recharge really is the path to greater engagement, in both life and work, just as Schwartz and Loehr noted in their book. In fact, the things we do as "play" can even become new interests that feed into our work.

Over the years, I've come to realize that my annual trip to Miraval is the only time when I can completely detach – or disengage – from my everyday life and focus on myself for an extended period of time. The purpose of this is not just to relax and let go (although this in itself is valuable), but also to spend time being self-reflective and self-aware. I get to know myself a little more each time I go, and I leave with new tools to help me navigate through life. By contrast, when at home, even if I decide to take a day off, there is always the pile of bills to pay, the laundry to be done, a phone or doorbell ringing, or someone needing something from me or preventing me from fully pulling away.

My annual trip to Miraval remains an "anchor" in my life. In other words, in the midst of chaos and change and stress and responsibility, I always have that to look forward to and to keep me steady. With the first several visits, I would feel sad when it was time to leave and almost count the days until my return, sometimes impatiently, even desperately at times. But having now absorbed the spirit of the place and made it part of my life, I celebrate every minute there, having learned to be very much in the moment. And when it is time to leave, I am accepting, knowing that I still have work to do in the world. I am no longer sad upon departure because I know I will return time and time again. I also have a little corner on my desk with things that remind me of Miraval

– photos, a small stone cairn, and a candle purchased there. This helps to keep me mindful in my daily activities and bring me back to the peace and tranquility of the place I have come to think of as a second home. This shrine of sorts also serves as an "anchor" in my life. And Joe? He looks forward to having a recharged and revved-up wife!

Fortunately, there are many lovely day spas and wellness centers in most communities, as well as meditation and other related classes. These provide an opportunity to schedule mini retreats and spa days all year long.

In spite of what I've written in this chapter, I don't want anyone to get the impression that they have to go to fancy spas or gyms or even get massages regularly in order to care for themselves. As a reminder, self-care includes a variety of activities such as creative pursuits, time alone, time with friends, and spending time in nature. It starts with acknowledging that you are just as important as those people and things that you care for and about. Taking time for yourself, in whatever form that might take, is not selfish or pampering, but rather routine maintenance for the body, mind, and spirit. It is just as important in our lives as eating, sleeping, and breathing. Self-care doesn't take anything away from others. Rather, it allows you to have more to give and to give in a more complete way. It keeps you healthy, happy, and fully engaged in life.

The life force has a natural rhythm of intake and output. Just as the sun rises and sets and the ocean ebbs and flows, so too must we create a system of regular energy renewal to balance energy expenditure. It must become the rhythm of our existence to create balance, harmony, health, and well-being. It's an ongoing process and something that has to become a natural part of our routine. Miraval, a local health club, and a book from a friend indoctrinated me into the rhythm of renewal and disengagement, and now I continue to honor myself – my most important asset – and my life by keeping it up all year long.

LESSONS LEARNED

---

1. Don't be someone who focuses on the price of everything but the value of nothing.

2. Make commitments, rather than excuses, to things that will support your own self-care.

3. When you open yourself up to change/new learning, the resources will appear.

4. Be alert to, and grateful for, "light sources" sent to illuminate your path.

5. The life force has a natural rhythm of intake and output. We must create a system of regular energy renewal to balance energy expenditure.

6. Disengagement and restoration allow us to function at our highest level physically and mentally.

7. There is comfort in talking to and spending time with others who share your challenges — no matter how devastating those challenges are.

8. We often need the help and support of others to encourage us to action, hold us accountable, support us, validate us, and partner with us.

9. We all find the time and money for the things that are important to us.

10. For women, girlfriends are so important.

11. Birthdays and milestones should be celebrated and are a chance to honor ourselves, to be good to ourselves, and to enjoy ourselves.

12. Self-care is not a luxury but rather routine maintenance for the body, mind, and spirit.

RECOMMENDED READING

Arylo, Christine. *Madly in Love with ME: The Daring Adventure of Becoming Your Own Best Friend*. Novato, CA: New World, 2012.

Loehr, Jim, and Tony Schwartz. *The Power of Full Engagement: Managing Energy, Not Time, is the Key to High Performance and Personal Renewal*. New York: Free Press, 2003.

Neff, Kristin. *Self-Compassion: The Proven Power of Being Kind to Yourself*. New York: HarperCollins, 2011.

RESOURCES

Miraval Resort & Spa www.MiravalResort.com

RETREATS

Empowered Woman, Enlightened Life™

Empowered Nurse, Enlightened Practice™

www.DonnaCardillo.com

chapter four

FINDING MY VOICE

A woman with a voice is by definition a strong woman.
But the search to find that voice can be remarkably difficult.

—MELINDA GATES

IN MY JUNIOR YEAR OF HIGH SCHOOL, I HAD AN ENGLISH teacher who preyed on the weak and those she didn't like. She was a short and stocky middle-aged woman with short-cropped gray hair and heavy, dark-rimmed glasses. In one class, she wrote a line from classic literature on the blackboard – something like, "To be, or not to be, that is the question." She asked for someone to interpret what it meant. Many hands shot up, but not mine. I felt incapable of abstract thought of this type. I tried to make myself invisible in her line of sight by perfectly lining up my silhouette with the person's in front of me. But like a feral dog, she could sense my fear and moved in for the kill. She called on me with a haughty bravado and an evil smirk on her face. I weakly pushed off my desk to a standing position and felt a wave of nausea overtake me. I looked at the sentence on the blackboard, which may as well have been written in a foreign language for all I understood of it. My mind began to race. Adrenaline gushed into my bloodstream like a fire hydrant being bled on a hot summer day. My body was rigid and my face burning hot.

I was in the last row of seats (I always tried to create as much distance between myself and this teacher as possible), so every other classmate now turned to look at me, their Catholic girls' school eyes piercing my flesh like thorns. I had nowhere to run or hide so, terrified, I sputtered out the best interpretation I could come up with. Silence hung in the air like a hangman's noose before an execution. My teacher slowly looked around at the class, paused, and said, not to me but to them, "That's the stupidest answer I have heard in my entire life." Her declaration further confirmed for me that I was intellectually inadequate. I remained intimidated by literature and related arts for years to come.

As a young woman, I was lacking what is often referred to as voice: the ability to express oneself well – one's thoughts, opinions, ideas, and needs – as well as to lead, inspire, persuade, and teach through that voice. In a 2012 report on gender equality and economic development, the World Bank defines voice as the ability to speak up and be heard, and to shape and share in discussions, discourse, and decisions. Acquiring voice demands an ongoing process of self-discovery, getting a handle on how the world works and where you fit in, building confidence, and mastering good communication skills. Based on these requirements and the above definition, I had my work cut out for me.

Although I'd always been a "talker," I never felt confident in my earlier life with formulating or conveying my point of view, having conversations with people I didn't know very well (or who were more educated than I was), asking for what I wanted or needed, or expressing my feelings. I often put my foot in my mouth; said really stupid things (I still do, on occasion); or expressed something in such an awkward, and occasionally inflammatory or crass, way that it was misconstrued. When it came to expressing myself in writing, I was even worse, at least in my own mind.

In my youth, while in conversation with others I would occasionally make up or exaggerate some minor details of my life or pretend to have done something I hadn't. For example, if someone whom I wanted to impress (or was intimidated by) asked me if I ever played golf, I might say yes, even though I hadn't. I just didn't feel I had enough to offer "on my own." Of course that is a dangerous road to go down because if asked a more specific question such as "Where have you played?" or "What type of clubs do you use?" I'd either have to make up another layer of falsehoods (which wouldn't sound credible, since I knew nothing about golf) or suddenly need to use the restroom. At some point, I think in my early twenties, I realized that this was not right and I had to stop doing it. Whatever you want to call it – lying, fibbing, falsehood, wearing a mask – I knew it was wrong and vowed to stop, which I did, cold turkey. In retrospect, I'm proud of myself for making that self-correction.

In other conversations, if a subject came up that I didn't know about or a concept was mentioned that was foreign to me, I would feign understanding and nod my head as if I knew what was being discussed. There were even occasions when the person bringing up the subject might look at me and say, "Are you familiar with that?" I would simply nod my head yes, too embarrassed to admit that I didn't, and pray that I wasn't asked for an opinion. If I was, another urgent trip to the restroom would probably be in order. I thought that if I asked a question or admitted that I didn't know something, my ignorance would show through and no one would be interested in talking to me.

I remember at least one occasion when I feigned understanding in a conversation and then the same subject came up again a few weeks later. I thought, *Damn – if only I had asked for an explanation last time, I'd actually know what this person was talking about this time.* Instead I felt naive and uncomfortable for the second time on the same subject. It finally occurred to me that it is better to be made uncomfortable once by asking a question and seeking knowledge than to remain in the dark for the rest of my life (keep in mind, this was pre-Internet, so when I ran to the restroom, I couldn't look up the word or the subject matter on my smartphone before returning to the conversation).

It's hard to know why I had a need to do this. I do remember that while growing up, I was constantly comparing myself to the very studious girls who had better grades, were always prepared to answer questions in class, and who seemed to be able to express themselves with quiet elegance. I, on the other hand, was often finishing my homework at the breakfast table on the morning that it was due, had no aspirations to achieve academic excellence as long as I passed everything, and was more interested in after-school activities than in history and English class. I assumed that some people were naturally intelligent and others were not, and I had clearly placed myself in the latter group. I also knew that my parents, neither of whom had the opportunity to go to college, had great respect and even reverence for people who were worldly and highly educated. I got the sense that those people were superior to us in some way. I always felt inadequate in the presence of people with college degrees until many years into my adulthood, after I achieved a few degrees of my own.

When I finally came to the realization, sometime in my early twenties, that the only way to stop being uneducated was to gain knowledge (duh!), I mustered up all the gumption I could and timidly started to say things like, "I'm not familiar with that term," or "I haven't heard that before. Can you tell me what it means?" The most amazing things began to happen when I did. Rather than people laughing at me, or walking away, or looking at me with disdain (as my insecure self feared), they would usually say something like, "Oh, I'm sorry. I should have explained myself." Or they would actually appear happy and enthusiastic to explain a concept to me. Eventually I let down my defenses and began to learn more, get more comfortable around other people, and actually enjoy acquiring new information this way. My world started to get a little bigger and my voice started to develop.

Back in high school, during senior English, with a different teacher, we were required to research a literary subject and write a paper on it. I chose to focus on Franz Kafka, whose writings often depicted a subject who found himself, much like I did, in a hopeless situation and doomed to failure. I did the research and created source cards in an accordion folder as we had been instructed. I then approached one of my more studious classmates and asked her to use my notes and references to write the paper for a fee (what we might call a ghostwriter today, but not an accepted practice in high school). She found my proposition intriguing and agreed to do it for fifty cents a page. I gladly paid her and she did a good job. As I write this, I pray there is no way anyone can go back and revoke my high school diploma for this deception. I didn't pay her to get out of doing the work. I paid her because I was certain I was completely incapable of writing an intelligent, coherent, and interesting paper.

It's so easy to hang onto our perceived shortcomings

rather than trying to get better at something. If I had asked my teacher or even this student to coach me on writing the paper, I likely could have learned something. But, as usual, I would have been afraid to let my ineptitude show through by asking for help. Rather than improve myself, I opted to put forward something false, and in essence to silence my own voice. I know now that it is never a good option, and it is a missed opportunity to learn, to grow, and to stretch.

Once I graduated from high school, I happily went off to a hospital-based nursing program. This type of program was often referred to as a "training" program for nurses, as opposed to a college program for nurses, the two choices available for nursing education at that time. I would be required to take numerous college-credit science courses as part of the program, as well as many other classroom-based nursing courses, but would not have a college degree upon completion. In fact, I wanted nothing to do with college or a degree at that time in my life. I wanted to roll up my sleeves and get out into the "real" world. This program had us in the hospital within the first few months to practice what we were learning in the classroom, and I was thrilled. A college-based program, at that time, might have delayed such clinical experience for a year or more. I had no patience for that.

Nursing was something I had decided on years prior, after working as a candy-striper in a hospital and falling in love with the rhythm, the pace, and the humanity of healthcare. I always loved science and helping people, so nursing seemed like the perfect career. Plus I wouldn't have to go to college to achieve it. What I didn't know at the time was that my career in nursing would afford me opportunities to gradually progress from a traditional clinical practice to being a manager in several private healthcare businesses, and even into a sales and training role for a healthcare education company. Each position required me to take on more responsibility, interact with a wider range of people, and learn how to conduct myself in a variety of situations. My confidence was growing as my experience broadened. My voice was getting stronger.

My foray into the world of professional speaking started in my late twenties when I was hired by a hospital in Secaucus, New Jersey, as the director of DRG (diagnostic related group) services. DRGs were a revolutionary new system created to determine how hospitals were reimbursed for care. But it wasn't a simple matter of dollars and cents. Payment would be tied into quality of care provided and other factors. There were many changes going on in healthcare at that time, and I had my hands full in my new position.

Three months into the job, my new boss told me he wanted me to speak to the physicians at their next monthly meeting about healthcare reimbursement and regulatory issues. I panicked at the mere thought of this, for many reasons. Like many others, I was a very reluctant public speaker. My only speaking experience at that time involved talking to grammar-school children about weight and nutrition while I was working at the weight control center and presenting in-service education to my coworkers in the emergency room. Plus, at that time I couldn't think of a more intimidating group to speak to, and I knew that the subject matter was something that both inflamed and irritated them. Physicians have always considered third-party payers (Medicare, Medicaid, insurance companies) as an interference with their practices.

I nervously told my boss I couldn't do it, rolling out every possible excuse I could think of, including that I was too new of an employee and the physicians didn't know me well enough yet nor I them, and that I needed more time to research the subject matter (I didn't feel I knew enough to do a presentation on the subject, even though I had been hired because of that knowledge). When I was done flinging excuses at him in a panicked, high-pitched voice (while flailing my arms and spewing salvia), he calmly and firmly asserted, "You *will* present to the physicians at this month's meeting." And that was that. He wasn't asking me; he was telling me. So in my mind I had two choices: I could either quit my new job (which I really liked) or speak to the physicians at their monthly meeting. I opted for the latter.

The big night came and I was more nervous than I'd been in my entire life to that point. The meeting was held in a top-floor conference room known as the Penthouse, which had floor-to-ceiling glass walls on two sides. Since this was an evening meeting, all I could see through the glass was the dark of night, making the whole experience more scary and ominous. The room was set up class-room-style, with about a hundred physicians in business suits seated in black plastic chairs, not unlike a wake. I wore my best conservative business suit – a taupe wool blend – with a white button-down collar, cotton blouse, and one of those floppy silk ties executive women were wearing in the 1980s, apparently to better blend in with their male counterparts. My stomach was twisted in knots, my legs felt like rubber, and I could feel the heat (and likely red blotches) rising from my chest onto my neck and face and scalp. I began to sweat profusely. I had brought handwritten notes with me and prayed that perspiration droplets would not drip onto the pages and blur the ink. I clung to the podium as a means of support in case I keeled over or my legs gave out. When I spoke, my voice was flat and quivering. My facial expression must have been blank with a touch of "controlled" panic. At least I didn't start crying.

As I looked out on the physicians, they all had equally flat expressions on their faces and looked like deer frozen by oncoming headlights. Just when I thought things couldn't get any worse, a doctor in the back row pulled out a pair of nail clippers and began trimming his fingernails! Because the room had good acoustics and was otherwise deathly silent except for the sound of my shaky voice, each click of the clippers reverberated and echoed through the room, causing my head to twitch to the side each time. I thought in horror (while still droning on robotically), *They're now so bored that they are grooming themselves! What next? Will they start flossing or passing the nail clipper around the room?*

I finally wrapped up my fifteen-minute presentation and asked the hardest question I ever had to ask in my life – "Does anyone have any questions?" – praying the whole time there wouldn't be any. One doctor raised his hand and asked a simple question that I was able to answer easily. I then said my good-byes and got out of that room as fast as my rubbery legs would take me.

I was mortified beyond words, assuming that I had bombed just as I "knew" I would. I was a former smoker and I went and found the nearest pack of cigarettes I could get my hands on (smoking was still allowed in hospitals then), borrowing a pack from a coworker. As I left work and drove home, I power-smoked for the next thirty minutes to make up for all the years I had abstained. My lungs and I had a lot of catching up to do.

I was now convinced that I had no choice but to both quit *and* leave the country. I had to get as far away from these people as I possibly could. I never wanted to see them again, or they me, I was certain. Of course relocation wasn't really an option, or a solution, but I did consider it for a few seconds! After discussing the whole ordeal with my husband Joe, I reluctantly opted to keep my job (if they would still have me) and face whatever would be waiting for me. I'd heard that with the passage of time, people forget and forgive, so I decided that I would keep a low profile for as long as possible until this whole incident was just a fading memory in the audience's mind.

I decided to arrive at work early the next day, sneak in the back door wearing dark clothes and oversized sunglasses, keep my head down, stay close to the wall, and slither into my office, quickly closing the door behind me. Surely I would be somewhat safe there, or at least isolated like a quarantined pathogen, until five p.m.

But my security bubble burst a short time later when there was a knock on my office door. My body became rigid with fear, and in a timid voice I called, "Yes?" The "interloper" announced, through the closed door, "It's Dr. Smith." A young and pleasant man, usually wearing a tweed blazer and khaki pants, he had been present for my doomed presentation. Was he here to tell me I'd made a complete fool of myself? There was no window in my office, so I had no way to escape. Plus he had heard my voice, so knew I was in there. I dutifully said, "Come in," praying that he would be gentle with his criticism.

Dr. Smith opened the door with a broad smile on his face (I remembered that people are often instructed to deliver bad news with a smile). He was jovial and friendly and said in an enthusiastic tone, "You gave a great presentation last night!" I studied his face for a moment to see if it appeared that he was being truthful. I also waited a moment to respond in case he was going to add "NOT!" He seemed sincere and eager for some response from me, so I said, in a stunned monotone, "I did?"

He continued, "Yes. You took a lot of complicated information and broke it down into easy-to-understand terms."

Like a parakeet that repeats the same phrase over and over, I repeated, "I did?"

He ended with an enthusiastic "Congratulations!" and went on his way.

I was frozen in place for a moment, processing what had just happened. It occurred to me that the only explanation was that he had seen how nervous I was during my speech and was just being nice to lessen my pain and embarrassment. I got up and closed the door (sealed the bubble) and started to do some work. A short time later there was another knock on the door. *So much for my self-imposed quarantine.* This time it was a physician with whom I had become somewhat friendly. He was grandfatherly in age and demeanor and spoke with a heavy Italian accent. In a slow, deep voice he declared, "I would have expected you to be nervous last night in front of those guys, but you were calm and cool as a cucumber. Congratulations . . . toughie!" (This physician continued to call me "toughie" for the remainder of my employment there, based on that one presentation.)

I'd barely had time to process this when yet another physician who had attended the presentation was standing in my doorway, smiling. He was one of the medical directors for the facility, tall and slender, always in a dark, expensive-looking suit and sporting a thin, almost black, Errol Flynn-style moustache. He, too, looked happy and said, "Hey, you're a good speaker!" I suddenly wondered if I was being tricked into a false sense of accomplishment before being summoned to the auditorium and given an award for the worst presentation in the hospital's history.

The parakeet in me chirped, "I am?"

"Yeah," he said. "Your voice carries, so I could hear you clearly all the way in the back of the room." He added, "And you enunciate your words clearly. Great job!" He strolled off and again I couldn't move, as if I'd just been hit with a stun gun. What was happening here?

I always knew that I had a loud booming voice and was very self-conscious about it. All my life people had been telling me to lower my voice or that I was busting their eardrums with my natural volume. Yet here was someone telling me that my "big mouth" was an asset. And no one had ever mentioned that I had good enunciation. Of course the secret to being successful is to take what you have and find a way to put it to good use. In my case, I eventually took what was originally a perceived drawback and turned it into as asset as a professional public speaker.

I came to realize, as a result of this one speaking experience, that audiences can rarely see how nervous you feel. That knowledge made me less self-focused in future presentations. I also discovered that you don't have to be the world's authority on a subject to impart some useful information to people – even to people with more education than you. Plus, you'll never know where your strengths and special talents lie unless you just get out there and try things, even at the risk of looking like a fool. Sometimes it's good to be pushed out of your comfort zone by others If left to our own devices, most of us wouldn't do much.

My new boss also stopped by the day after my debut presentation. With a satisfied look on his face and a slight nod, he told me I did a good job. He said it in a way that communicated to me that he'd never expected anything different from me. I could tell that he was pleased, and that was a great relief to me. From then on, on a regular basis, he would ask me to speak on similar subjects to hospital directors, new hires, the board of directors, and even out in the community. I was surprised but thrilled when he made mention of my "strong" public speaking skills on my annual employee evaluation that year and subsequent years as well.

The more I spoke in front of audiences and got some positive feedback here and there, the more comfortable I became. When I did presentations for staff members at my hospital shortly after speaking to the physician group, I began getting stronger accolades and gradually started to become more animated while speaking, able to inject some levity into what could often be a dry subject, and to feel more at ease in front of audiences. The more natural and relaxed I became with the medium, the more genuine my delivery and my message. Regular public speaking also brought out the entertainer and stand-up comic in me, not to mention the educator, which was all very satisfying and enjoyable.

Besides public speaking, my managerial role at this hospital, as well as leadership roles I held in various professional associations at the time, also required that I take an active role in – and sometimes facilitate – meetings, participate in interdisciplinary discussions, and learn to have civil discourse with parties both in and out of my place of employment. I gradually began to master all of this, thereby strengthening my own voice, by observing and modeling others who were good at it, by reading books and articles on how to communicate effectively, and sometimes by trial and error. This led to a greater sense of self-awareness, confidence, and personal power, not to mention the respect and admiration of my peers.

All of those years of public speaking in the hospital, I had been "winging it," doing things from behind the podium as I thought they should be done, but not based on any real knowledge of what made a good presentation. Years later, when I decided to speak for a living, I began to make a study of the craft of speaking. How? By going down to the good old public library and reading books on how to speak well in public. I also watched videos of great speakers to observe their style, timing, storytelling skill, body movement, audience interaction, and so on. There is so much technique involved, more than I could have ever imagined! I learned that experience alone is not the best teacher where public speaking is involved. In fact, if you rely on experience alone without studying the craft of speaking, you are simply polishing your mistakes. I wanted to be – in fact, needed to be – as good as I could get.

I also eventually joined the National Speakers Association and began networking with some of the world's most effective communicators. I learned so much just from observing them presenting at conventions and at meetings. When there's something you want to do, it makes sense to rub elbows with those who are successfully doing that thing.

When I started my seminar business, I obviously planned to do some speaking, but I had no thoughts of writing. I was still in the "I may be able to master public speaking, but I will never be able to write" mindset. But after a few years of speaking, prospective clients and colleagues started asking me, "What have you had published?" I was aghast. There was an expectation that, as an educator, I would also write and publish. If anyone had told me this going into the speaking business, I probably would have chosen another path. So I realized, with a great deal of dread, that if I wanted to continue as a speaker and an educator, I was going to have to try my hand at writing for publication.

I thought it would be a good idea to start small and simple and keep it close to home. After all, I didn't want to embarrass myself on a national level. So the first question was: what to write about? I had always heard, "Write about what you love; write about what you know." After having read every classic and contemporary book on the art of résumé writing and then teaching those concepts to nurses for several years, I decided to write a short piece, which I titled "The 5 Do's and Don'ts of Résumé

Writing for Nurses." A "do's and don'ts" article is one of the simplest to write and can be used for almost any subject: knitting, childrearing, quilt making. It's not meant to be comprehensive coverage of the subject but rather to provide some short and succinct tips. More importantly, it didn't take a lot of creative writing skill on my part.

I created some bullet points of information and wrote a simple opening and close. Now that the article was written, whom could I get to publish it? I decided to contact the editor of a small, simple newsletter (two black-and-white photocopied pages with a staple in the upper-left-hand corner) of a small local chapter of a nursing professional association I belonged to. I didn't know the editor personally, but I gave her a call. I introduced myself as a member and told her I'd written an article. Before I could even get all the details out she said, "The deadline's the fifteenth. Can you have it to me by then?" *Wow*, I thought. This was easier than I'd imagined it would be. I even flattered myself by thinking that perhaps she had heard of me and my seminars and was therefore eager to publish my "work." My ego was quickly deflated when I realized, by her somewhat aloof and perfunctory tone, that she didn't know who I was but was simply desperate for content (as most association newsletter editors are). She had space to fill and would probably have published almost anything somewhat literate at that point in time. I suppose she did have some standards, though, and apparently my little article met hers.

So I got my first article published — if you can even call it that — and was quite tickled. I don't know if anyone ever read it, but that didn't matter to me. The fact that I had written something that got into print was thrilling, no matter how small the scale. So I decided to take it to the next level!

Reflecting on writing about "something you love," I decided to write about listening to recorded books, something I had recently begun doing. I would borrow books on CD from the library and listen to them while driving, exercising, etc. I loved the experience; I was able to get more "reading" in, and I found it easier to listen to some books rather than read them, especially business books. So I decided to write a short piece about all that. This time I contacted the editor of my business owners' association newsletter — a four-color, four-page printed newsletter — a step up! Once again, the editor seemed desperate for content and happily published my article after doing some minor editing of it. (Thank goodness for editors!)

At the next chapter meeting of that association, one of the members came up to me and said, "Hey, I read that article you wrote in the newsletter about listening to recorded books. I'd been thinking about doing that, so I got myself down to the library after reading your piece and borrowed some. I'm really enjoying the experience. Thanks for writing the article!" *Wow,* I thought. *Maybe there's something to this writing thing!* This member didn't say, "You're a great writer. You have a literary future!"

She said, in essence, that something I wrote created positive action on her part and had enriched her life in some way. I was beginning to understand the power of the written word and the agency of my developing voice.

I was on a roll . . . or so I thought. I decided to write an article about getting started in business, the obstacles I overcame, and so on. I submitted it to what I saw as the pinnacle of publishing at the time, *Nursing Spectrum* magazine (now Nurse.com). I mailed in my article and query letter, and within one short week I received an envelope in the mail from them! I was bursting with excitement. I hadn't been sure I would ever hear back from them, never mind in such a short period of time. So I ripped open the envelope with joyful anticipation and began to read the letter. I quickly realized it was the dreaded "rejection letter." My excitement turned into disappointment. I was crushed. I was devastated. I was embarrassed. The negative self-talk started up at full volume: "Who do you think you are? Whatever made you think you could write? You must have been crazy to think you could get something published in such a prestigious publication." I vowed that day that I would never write again. I felt like such a fool. I didn't want to re-experience that sense of rejection. I could just see my high school English teacher throwing her head back with laughter and cackling, "I could have told you that and saved you the trouble." Her reference to my being "stupid" echoed in my head.

About a week later, I picked up the letter again and

read it all the way though this time. (The first time around I only got to the part where the editor said they couldn't publish it.) The editor had been kind enough to give me tips on how to improve the article and encouraged me to rework and resubmit it at a later time. That was very generous and gracious of her. But I eventually realized that this particular article was too much about me – too self-serving – and decided to scrap it.

What I did next, and should have done in the beginning but didn't know any better, was to go down to the public library and borrow books on how to write for publication, how to contact editors, how to edit your own work, what makes for good reading, and so on. I also started to study articles in the magazines I wanted to write for. I noticed how they started with a statement to introduce the topic and make it relevant to the reader. I observed how the ending summarized and wrapped things up. I noted how the body was organized. I was beginning to learn the art and the science of writing for publication. I also began to realize that it's not a matter of either having or not having "talent." Instead, by studying and working on the craft, along with possessing a strong desire to learn, anyone can dramatically improve her ability to write and express herself well.

I eventually learned how to write well enough that I became a regular columnist for the very magazine/website that sent me my first rejection letter – the letter that easily could have kept me from ever writing again. I have since published over two hundred articles, and written four books and countless blog posts. I mention this not to boast but to illustrate how easy it would have been for me to never develop this part of myself after receiving that first rejection letter. I know that rejection has stopped others from writing. Who knew there was a writer hiding inside of me? It took decades of living before it came out. Regular writing allowed me to get comfortable with the medium, perfect the art of expressing my views, and become clearer with my language and style of communication. I was giving voice to my growing expertise by communicating my knowledge in writing.

I now know that getting rejection letters is a rite of passage in the writing world. I always say to budding writers or those who wish to publish, "When you get your first rejection letter," not "If you get a rejection letter," because it goes with the territory. So when you get your first rejection letter, shout it from the rooftops. It signifies that you have made the effort to write and submit something and that it has been acknowledged! Celebrate it. Frame it. Tell your friends and family about it. Because the real power is in the doing, not in the outcome. We become a little more alive each time we step out of our comfort zone and take a risk. We draw strength, confidence, and experience by acting rather than hesitating. Some people want to quit as soon as something seems hard or they can't do it perfectly right away. But there is arrogance in the belief that you could become really good at something with minimal effort, time, or experience. Humble yourself to learning, stick with it, and keep moving forward. It's never about the destination but rather who you become along the journey.

Every woman has something entirely unique to say and teach, and must develop her own voice. But I don't want you to think that you must get published or speak in public, as there are many other ways to achieve this. Here are a few ideas: Join a club or association and get on a committee where you will be asked for your input and opinion. Work with a coach or counselor to help you find the words to stand up for yourself in difficult situations. Take a class on creative writing and get group feedback on your work. Join Toastmasters to learn the art of oral self-expression and build confidence. Attend a support group and tell your story in a supportive environment. Start asking for what you want in small ways initially, such as asking for a better table at a restaurant or a late check out at a hotel. Do some of the writing exercises in the books referenced at the end of this chapter, such as *Write It Down, Make It Happen* and *Writing Down the Bones*. Most if not all of these things will be hard for many and will require learning, courage, and perseverance. But the journey to find and develop your voice is an ongoing one and will lead to a more satisfying and productive life.

My own process of developing my voice received a huge boost when I decided to enter graduate school as an adult, an experience I'll discuss in depth in chapter 5. At the time, the nature of my business was pushing me to write, and I feared that graduate school would, too. I was not wrong about this, but the writing and thinking I was forced to do in graduate school turned out to be an amazing gift. Graduate school is where I really started to develop my own unique style of writing and a growing ability to express myself. I was required to form opinions and defend them, to do research on subjects that were of interest to me, and to write and speak about it all. I can still recall getting one of my first papers back and my professor commenting that I had a "good conversational style of writing." I remember thinking incredulously: *I have a style? And it's a "good" style?* This created a new-found confidence and encouraged my future writing. Once again, a little positive feedback from someone I looked up to made a big difference in my life.

By the time I graduated, I was more articulate and literate. My "voice" was getting stronger and more clearly defined. I was becoming aware of my unique perspective. Instead of feeling ignorant and unworthy when I opened a newspaper, went to a party with people I didn't know, or talked to people more experienced or educated than I was, I formulated opinions on specific world events and social issues and was not afraid to share them. To my surprise, I found that people reacted to my opinions not with antagonism and disagreement, but with admiration, even when they didn't exactly share my views. In fact, many people began to seek my advice and input on a variety of subjects related to my experience and background. I felt more empowered, self-assured, and in control of my life and decisions. I even felt happier.

In recent years, I've come to appreciate an entirely new way that writing can contribute to finding my voice. For a high school reunion four years ago, I dug into old memorabilia and came across a compendium of original student poetry and artwork that my schoolmates used to put together each year. I was absolutely shocked to find two poems of mine there. I had completely forgotten about them. And even though they were simple I was surprised that I'd had the gumption to write and submit them. It made me consider that when my defenses were down and I temporarily ignored the negative voices in my head, I was capable of more than I gave myself credit for. Discovering those poems made me ask myself some questions about my writing practice in the present day. Perhaps I had been holding my own creative side hostage and needed to negotiate a release. Not long after, I wrote a short spontaneous poem and was startled at what flowed through the keyboard onto the screen. Even though I had become a writer, I was still convinced that I could never write poetry or fiction. These days, I'm starting to rethink that and am willing to try. Just as a sculptor or portrait painter needs to start somewhere and learn and master basic technique before creating a masterpiece, so too does a writer of any type, whether fiction, memoir, articles, poetry, and so on.

Of course writing for publication is one thing. But I discovered that writing for my eyes only could be a powerful tool of self-discovery. Poet Cecil Day-Lewis said, "We do not write in order to be understood, we write in order to understand." The very act of writing helps me to find the words (my voice), clarify my thoughts, and get to know myself. It is also a way to let go of certain things that no longer serve me and make way for new energy. Today, I accomplish all this through journaling, blogging, writing letters to myself and others – whether I plan to send them or not – and even writing my own stories and memoir. This type of life-writing is something I recommend for all women.

Telling my stories, even privately, has the potential to help me revisit a time or place in my life in a new way, work through pain, gain new insights, and even resolve and leave behind issues from the past. It is also a means to leave a legacy, unburden myself, and when done publicly, teach and inspire. There are things I still have trouble talking about, and those are some of the things I write about in my journal, my books, and my blogs and articles. Since broaching vulnerable aspects of my life can be scary, writing about those difficult issues can serve as a gateway to seeing them more clearly and sometimes finding solutions if they are unresolved, or just being able to let them go. Doing it privately can also be a first step to later talking or writing about these subjects in public.

One example of writing from a place of vulnerability was the telling of the story of my first marriage in chapter 2 of this book. I had never written about my first marriage, and on the rare occasions that I spoke about it, it was clear that I still harbored some hurt and angry feelings toward my ex. As I was recalling and writing the details, I realized that many of my own family members didn't know all that I went through during that time, since I had never fully revealed it to anyone. Exploring through writing that painful and difficult time in my life, I was able to revisit it through the eyes of the woman I am now, not the girl-woman I was then – the one who lacked a voice, confidence, and a sense of self. I gained a new perspective on the events that transpired and saw everything more clearly and objectively. Through writing honestly about it, I no longer felt like a victim. I was able to make peace with what happened – what some might call closure – and let it go. I even felt some compassion for my ex-husband and what he must have been going through at that time. I realized it is simply one chapter – literally and figuratively – in my life's story, and a key component in bringing me to where I am now.

When starting this book, although I'd already written three career-related books for nurses, well over a hundred articles, and a daily advice column and blogs, I had very little idea of how to approach writing a memoir, which is a unique art form. Whenever I get stuck or need help with a project or have a desire to learn more about something, I still go down to the good old brick-and-mortar public library. I tap out my needs/wants on the keyboard into the subject bar of the computer catalog and wait to see what treasures will be revealed to me. This time, while struggling with writing this book, I discovered the wonderful little book *The Memoir Project: A Thoroughly Non-Standardized Text for Writing & Life,* by Marion Roach Smith. I learned so much after just a few pages that I went out and bought my own copy. Even though I am a very experienced writer, I once again had to humble myself to learning this form of self-expression that was new to me.

When I tell the story today of that junior high school teacher who implied I was stupid, people often ask me if I ever went back to show her what I have accomplished. I haven't, and I have no interest in doing so. I have nothing to prove to her because I realize that her response to me that day was based on her need to intimidate and criticize, and was not a genuine response to a young woman whom she was charged with educating. But I did have something to prove to myself over the years: that I had something of value to contribute to the world and was able to convey it in a meaningful way. I had to stretch myself beyond my perceived limits to gain some level of competency and skill in public speaking, writing, and just expressing myself well in any situation. The risks I took, personally and professionally, humbling myself to learning, taking steps to get as good as I could get, and continuing on that journey today, were some of the most worthwhile actions I have taken. Why? Because once you find and develop your voice, there's nothing you can't do. Like the Melinda Gates quote at the beginning of this chapter implies, finding my voice has made me a strong woman – someone who is self-aware, stands up for herself, is not afraid to speak out on things she believes in and is passionate about, believes she has something of value to contribute to the world, and is willing to do so. It has given me the opportunity to tell my own truth and better understand myself and my experiences. It has allowed me to teach, inspire, lead, persuade, comfort, and even make a living. It has provided a means for me to be a voice for others who have not yet found their voice or do not yet have the tools for self-expression. And what is all that worth? I can think of very little that means more to me.

LESSONS LEARNED

1. Acquiring voice demands an ongoing process of self-discovery.

2. Writing is a powerful form of self-expression, whether shared with others or kept private.

3. Writing is a way to better understand oneself.

4. Anyone can dramatically improve her ability to speak in public and write for publication with some education, self-study, coaching, and experience.

5. Although self-expression can make one feel vulnerable, it is also an opportunity for validation, unburdening (letting go), and being a vehicle for others who cannot express themselves.

6. It's so easy to hang onto our perceived shortcomings rather than trying to get better at something.

7. You'll never know where your strengths and special talents lie unless you just get out there and try things, even at the risk of looking like a fool.

8. A little positive feedback goes a long way, so be sure to give it whenever you can and appreciate it when it comes your way.

9. The real power is in the doing — not in the outcome.

10. It is often good to be pushed beyond our perceived limits by others. If left to our own devices, most of us wouldn't do much.

11. When there's something you want to do, it makes sense to rub elbows with those successfully doing that thing or those who have already made the journey.

12. By developing our own voice, we give voice to others.

13. Write for yourself. Write for others. Just write.

RECOMMENDED READING

Cameron, Julia. *The Artist's Way: A Spiritual Path to Higher Creativity*. New York: Tarcher/Putnam, 1992.

Carnegie, Dale. *The Quick and Easy Way to Effective Speaking: Modern Techniques for Dynamic Communication*. New York: Dale Carnegie & Associates, 1962. Reprint, New York: Pocket, 1990.

Goldberg, Natalie. *Writing Down The Bones: Freeing the Writer Within*. 2nd ed. Boston: Shambhala, 2005.

Klauser, Henriette Anne. *Write It Down, Make It Happen: Knowing What You Want and Getting It*. New York: Touchstone, 2000.

Lamott, Anne. *Bird by Bird: Some Instructions on Writing and Life*. New York: Anchor, 1995.

Sandberg, Sheryl. *Lean In: Women, Work and the Will to Lead*. New York: Knopf, 2013.

Smith, Marion Roach. *The Memoir Project: A Thoroughly Non-Standardized Text for Writing & Life*. New York: Grand Central, 2011.

RESOURCES

The National Speakers Association www.nsaspeaker.org

Toastmasters International www.toastmasters.org

chapter five

WAKING SLEEPING BEAUTY

Be patient with yourself. Self-growth is tender;
it's holy ground. There is no greater investment.

—STEPHEN COVEY

THE MORE I WENT OUT INTO THE WORLD, THE MORE I FELT compelled to improve myself intellectually, physically, and emotionally. If I was going to rub elbows with the movers and shakers of the world and possibly become one of them myself, I was going to need to do a lot of building, chiseling, and buffing to create a confident, healthy, and whole human being. The impetus for change came a few years after my business started. I attended a local National Association of Women Business Owners dinner meeting and learned about something that would change my life in unanticipated ways.

That evening's presenter was a professor from a local university who spoke about communication skills. He brought brochures along for a new master's program that the university was launching in the fall, an MA in corporate and public communication. I looked at the required courses and noticed that the degree appeared to be tailor-made for me: public speaking, professional writing, public relations, healthcare communication, etc. I got excited just reading the brochure!

Like many people with an undergraduate degree (I had earned a BS in healthcare management ten years prior, about twelve years after my nursing education), I had occasionally thought about going back for a master's degree, but could never find a program that really interested me. Of course, that's also a great excuse to procrastinate about going back: "I *would* go back to school but just don't know what I want to major in." I had considered many different courses of study for graduate school including nursing, education, and public health, but none of them really grabbed me . . . until now.

It occurred to me that if they were just starting the program in the fall (it was currently springtime), I had better enroll right away, before they got their act together, because, I hoped, they'd accept *anyone* who applied early just to fill the class. I didn't see myself as graduate school material or think I would have a good chance of getting into a program under "normal" circumstances. Once I was in, hopefully they'd forgive my self-antici-pated academic shortcomings and say, "Push her through. She was one of the first ones to sign up and we need the testimonials!" In other words, I thought I had to find their weak spot in order to get accepted into, and eventually graduate from, the program. And since I recognized that there was a narrow window of opportunity to do this before the program launched, and that such an opportunity might never come along again, I impulsively applied. I didn't do it for my business. I did it for myself. I believe that I had a deep-seated desire to develop my intellect, but had often held myself back out of the belief that I just wasn't smart enough. This time, I decided to hop on the train and see where it took me.

It was not that I had any extra time to attend school. I was scheduled to the max between running my business, looking after my husband and family, taking care of my home, and just trying to get through each day. But we always make time for those things that are truly important to us. Once you make a commitment to something, just as I did when I decided to start my business and then to return to school, you miraculously "find" a way to make it happen.

I did not have any extra money for school, either. In fact, our household income was minimal at that time. I had recently started the business and was still struggling to earn a living from it. I was investing any profits back into the business. My husband's disability had progressed to the point that he was no longer able to work. He had no disability insurance and had been turned down for Social Security disability benefits, which often happens – we were told – the first time many people with MS apply. Joe had a small pension from a prior job and I had a meager income from the antiques business, but we had started to dip into our savings.

After what I perceived as my miraculous acceptance into the master's program, my first tuition bill came due. Now it was time to finance my education. I had planned to apply for student loans, like so many others do, and pay them off for the rest of my life. But I was dumbfounded to learn that I was required to be taking at least six credits (two courses) per semester to qualify for these loans. I could only manage one three-credit course each semester in terms of time commitment and financial outlay for books and so on, and even that would be a heavy load for me to carry. I had to find another way to pay for school. Where there is a will, I told myself, there is always a way.

I went online and started to search for scholarship money, something I had not needed to do earlier in my life. I eventually found a scholarship offered by the National Speakers Association (NSA), of which I was a member. The scholarship was for full-time students of speech or communication. I had one requirement covered (my major), but the "full-time" part was not going to happen. So, disappointed, I put the application aside and continued desperately to search. A few weeks later I noticed that the NSA application due date was approaching and decided that I had nothing to lose by submitting it. The worst that could happen was that they would say no. On the other hand, if I didn't apply at all, I was guaranteed to get nothing.

This application required that I write a brief essay about why I needed/wanted the scholarship. I wrote about how I wished I could be a full-time student and what a luxury that would be for me. But as the main support of my family, I was only able to take one course at a time, yet I still needed the money. The NSA awarded an additional scholarship that year just for me, in addition to the usual ones they award to full-time students. I was moved to tears when the surprise announcement was made at a national convention. I was there to receive the good news and the check. This allowed me to pay for most of my first year of school.

During my second year of grad school, one of my professors, who knew of my personal struggles, nominated me for an Executive Women of New Jersey scholarship, which I received. That award even included an allowance for living expenses. It came at a time when I was certain I would have to put my schooling on hold for lack of funds. It provided the additional financial support I needed to complete my education. Help and support of all types are everywhere if you seek them out.

After being awarded that first scholarship that required recipients to be full-time students, which I was not, I began to realize that almost everything in life, including some scholarship requirements, is negotiable. Additionally, the experience reminded me that if you don't ask, you don't get. You have nothing to lose by asking for what you want and need. There's an old adage that goes: "If you don't ask, then the answer is always no."

I have since learned, through my writing and research, that there is much more scholarship money available, from many sources, than most of us realize. Lack of personal funds should never be an obstacle to going back to school, or doing anything else you want to do, for that matter. When people say to me, "I can't afford that," regarding something they deeply want to do or have, I suggest that they change the statement to a question and say, instead, "*How* can I afford that?" It reframes the situation and sets you on a path toward a solution.

Once I entered grad school, my mind began to expand in ways I could never have imagined. Parts of my brain that had been dormant for decades began to wake up. I was learning about organizational theory, scholarly and commercial writing, corporate training and development, the art of rhetoric, and more. I started forming opinions about things I previously knew very little about and became more conversant on a variety of subjects related to social issues, politics, current events, business, and even healthcare. The paradox of education is that the more you learn, the more you discover there is to learn. The most significant thing was that I started to learn more about myself. I began to have more confidence and, as mentioned in chapter 4, was developing my "voice."

While I was still in school, my newly acquired education was a wave that was propelling me into the future. It seemed that I no sooner took a required course in something such as corporate training and development than my first corporate training opportunity came along. After learning how to write a research-based article as part of my coursework, I was asked by a prestigious nursing publication to write such an article – the type where you search scholarly journals and quote the current literature. I would have had no idea how to do that if I hadn't been in grad school at the time, and I likely would have either turned down the opportunity or looked inept trying.

From the outset, the thought of completing graduate school was overwhelming. How could I ever get through the thirty-three credits required to complete the degree, especially since I had to take only one course at a time? To cope, I had to focus only on getting through the current course, rather than projecting into the future. Then I'd focus on the next course, and so on. I knew that if I kept at it, I'd eventually get to the end. And I did. It reminded me of the old riddle: "How do you eat an elephant? One bite at a time."

It took me five years to finish that degree. Why five years? Because that's the maximum amount of time the school allowed. I chipped away at the degree and was on the slow track all the way while fellow students were whizzing by me at lightning speed. But when considering starting, I thought, *Five years is going to pass whether I'm in school or not. At the end of that five years I can either have a degree or still be thinking about it.* I'm so glad I took the plunge!

On graduation day, I was sitting in my cap and gown next to another woman who had started the program at the same time I did. She and I were the last students to graduate from that original class. The whole thing was so surreal to me. I leaned over and whispered to her, "I can't believe that I am about to have a master's degree bestowed upon me. I always thought that only really smart people got master's degrees." And I had never thought of myself that way. She looked at me and whispered back, "You *are* a really smart person." Her words caused me to sit up a little taller, feel a little more confident, and straighten my mortarboard.

For me, this graduation was like the scene from *The Wizard of Oz* when the Scarecrow finally meets the wizard. Throughout the movie, the Scarecrow always feels inadequate because he perceives that he doesn't have a brain. I say "perceives" because he is quite capable of intelligent conversation, planning, and execution; he just lacks confidence. But at the end of the movie, the wizard tells the Scarecrow that the only difference between him and great scholars is a diploma, as he ceremoniously hands him a ribbon-tied scroll. Suddenly, with diploma in hand, the Scarecrow begins to think great thoughts, articulate eloquently, and solve complex equations. That's what my diploma did for me; it validated that I had a brain in my head, and that has made all the difference in my life. It made me a better version of myself. I didn't decide to go back to school because I thought it would help my business or my work or because anyone was telling me I needed to. I did it for myself. Education is a gift you give yourself. I say to anyone, regardless of your background or future plans, go back to school for yourself first; everything else is secondary.

I hear others offer a million excuses why they won't or don't go back to school. Now that I am on the "other side" of higher education, I can say it is not something to fear but rather something to embrace. It is a stepping-stone to self-actualization – an awakening, a blossoming, a real opening of the mind, a portal. I love this quote by philosopher John Dewey: "Education is not preparation for life; education is life itself."

After graduation I had a greater sense of confidence and felt better able to contribute to the world around me. And just as important, I was able to more fully participate in my own life. I was slowly becoming more alive. There is a Russian proverb that goes, "Education is light, lack of it darkness." I was creating more openings for the light to pour in. Or was I allowing my own internal light new avenues to be released? Probably a little of both.

In *A New Earth*, Eckhardt Tolle says, "Your inner purpose is to awaken. It is that simple." I was certainly working on just that. I started to feel as though I was awakening from a lifelong trance – a trance of hiding all of who I really was, fearing that I was so imperfect and inadequate that I needed to remain in hiding, hiding in plain sight. It was a trance of fear, self-doubt, and insecurity that had dulled my essence and repressed my true nature for much of my life. My intellectual awakening helped me to better understand the world around me and make more sense of it. It opened me up to new ways of thinking and seeing things. What I didn't realize then is that it would also be a stepping-stone toward my spiritual awakening.

A trance is the antithesis of being fully alive and awake. I think of the old zombie movies of the 1950s and '60s and remember bodies that walked around in a robotic way, disengaged from life, going through the motions, operating on autopilot. Their eyes were open, but they didn't really see. For me it's always been so easy to overindulge in food (others use alcohol or drugs) or zone out on television, electronic devices, and excessive sleep at times. I now see all of this as avoidance of knowing myself, embracing all parts of myself, and testing my limits; in other words, living and working to my highest potential. I eventually had to confront the question that we all must ask ourselves: How alive do I want to be?

Shortly after finishing grad school, and about eight years after starting my business, I experienced a perceptible shift in my inner life – those internal thoughts, feelings, beliefs, and attitudes that you base your life on, that govern your actions, that create your priorities. It felt like the tectonic plates inside of me were shifting, getting ready to create mountains, volcanoes, and even new continents. In hindsight, I have no doubt that my educational experience was fueling this change. Additionally, a few years later when I read the wonderful book by Angeles Arien, *The Second Half of Life*, I realized that this "shift" occurred during my fiftieth year of life; no coincidence, I'm sure. Here was yet another major shift at the start of a new decade. This decade was to mark my spiritual awakening, my true "becoming."

Around this time, it seemed that new information, new experiences, and new people were coming into my life like a monsoon rain that turns deserts into lush green plains. As an example, I was drawn to a women's weekend business retreat, one where the main focus was setting goals and planning for the future. Initially I hesitated to go, reluctant to spend the money and carve out the time. But going to graduate school had taught me to make it happen, or as I like to say, just show up for life. That's when the magic happens. So I signed up.

At the retreat I met a participant who was a life and fitness coach. Fitness coaches are different from personal trainers, who create exercise programs for you and coach you in person through workout sessions. By contrast, fitness coaches don't train you but work with you, often by phone, to mentor and guide you to create a healthy lifestyle. Since I was struggling with my weight, I decided to work with her for a few months. She helped me to gain some perspective on my hectic life, made me aware of how sedentary I was on days spent in the office at the computer, and stressed the need to just take some time off periodically.

I recorded in my journal what I had relayed to this coach about the shift I was experiencing:

I feel as though I have crossed a bridge – one that fell away after I crossed it – so there is no going back. It is like opening two large doors into a secret garden – a lush garden filled with fresh air – one that I didn't know existed. At times I feel less of this earth and more of another plane.

A subsequent journal entry:

I feel the hardened, gnarly, scarred, faded crust cracking and a brand new smooth, radiant, vibrant being emerging. It's time to let go of the past – to drop the ballast that has held me back, slowed me down. Look out world, here I come!

Having joined the gym mentioned in Chapter 3 several months prior, which was now helping to keep my stress under control and had improved my energy and outlook, I signed up for an intensive four-week workout class intended to bolster my fitness and weight-loss goals. The class leader, Michele, would become another light source in my life. After her class was over, I signed on to work one-on-one with her as a personal trainer. We would chat during our sessions and found that we had a mutual interest in all things metaphysical. Although "metaphysics" was not a word in my vocabulary at that time, I came to learn that it is used to describe those experiences that go beyond the physical or lie outside of objective experience. In other words, we both believed that there was more to life, death, and our own existence than science had hard data for. Even though we're decades apart in age, we connected on a deep soul level.

During one of our conversations, Michele relayed two profound experiences she had had with a Reiki practitioner. She talked about how this individual worked with chakras and energy balancing – all things I had never heard of. Although I was a bit skeptical about it all, I felt compelled to contact this therapist and make an appointment. When I arrived, the practitioner explained about energy centers (chakras) and pathways (meridians) in the body and how they can become blocked, causing us to hold onto negative energy and impeding our creativity. Although I didn't necessarily buy into it all, I decided to just go with the flow. Sometimes you have to trust the process and open yourself up to things that you may not yet understand.

The Reiki session consisted of the practitioner lightly placing her hands on different areas of my body and at other times holding her hands just above. I was fully clothed, lying down on her treatment table with my eyes closed. With soft background music playing, I fell into a deep state of relaxation.

Within a few minutes, my breathing changed. I became aware of taking intermittent, short, staccato breaths. I felt like I couldn't get enough air into my lungs. It reminded me of when I was a child and afraid of the dark and during the night, either in a dream state or in an awake state – I'm not sure which – I would sometimes cry and sob so hard I could hardly breathe.

After the session, the therapist said that my energy had been very blocked. She talked about all the emotional stuff I had been holding onto and how my excess body weight was part of that and created a protective barrier. Wow – this was more than I bargained for! She said she sensed that I needed a good cry. That was so true, and how interesting that I had a memory during the session of sobbing in childhood. She also said that she had been praying during the session and asking all of my relatives both alive and dead to rally around me so I didn't feel so alone in my caregiving. (Although I had mentioned to her that I was caregiver, I didn't elaborate on my state of mind.) That really touched a nerve, and I almost burst out crying at that moment, but I held it back. It seems I had gotten into a habit of holding a lot of things back. Even though I had regained some energy and enthusiasm for my business after my last crisis of self, the burden of caregiving plus the ongoing grief over my husband's illness was just under the surface. We talked for a little while longer, and when I left her office I felt physically and emotionally lighter. My coat even felt big on me, as if I had shed some pounds in the process.

The next morning I got up, had breakfast, and was at my computer by seven a.m. as usual to start my day's work. Suddenly I felt an overwhelming compulsion to meditate. That had never happened to me before. Years earlier, I had been reluctantly initiated into Transcendental Meditation – a very specific meditation discipline – to appease my first husband when he decided he wanted to try it. And while I did learn to meditate at that time and found great peace in the practice (that is one gift my ex did give me), I never kept up with it. I had tried on numerous occasions over the years to get back into it, to no avail.

On this morning after my first Reiki session, I tried to resist this pull to meditate. It felt like an energetic and relentless toddler tugging on my shirtsleeve, insistent on getting my attention. How dare anyone or anything get in the way of my ritualistic (bordering on cult-like) communing with my beloved electronica first thing every morning! I attempted to distract myself with work. When that didn't do the trick I closed my eyes for a few minutes and tried to refocus, thinking "the urge" might go away. I then tried again to get back to work unsuccessfully. The pull was too strong. And just as often happens with a nagging child, I realized that the only way I would get any relief was to give in. The balance of power shifted and I finally got up (I really felt as if I had no choice), went to a quiet space in my home, and meditated with ease for thirty minutes. That evening I felt compelled to meditate again and did so for another thirty minutes. I began meditating twice a day for weeks. I barely had to think about it. It just became part of my routine.

There are so many myths and misconceptions about meditation. I eventually learned more about it from reading books and attending workshops. While there are many different meditation disciplines, it is not necessary to empty one's mind of thoughts, as some people believe. That may be the goal of some practitioners, but for most of us, that would be difficult to achieve because the mind is made to think. In the mindfulness form of meditation that I practice, the purpose is to focus the mind, usually on the breath. I become very aware of the process of inhaling and exhaling, how my torso expands and contracts, and the feel of the cool air entering my nostrils and then the same air, now warmed by my lungs, escaping. I am aware of any thoughts that pop up in my mind during this time, but I "practice" not judging those thoughts and just letting them go like leaves floating down a gentle stream. Even the most devout practitioners struggle with meditation. But that is why it is called a practice.

Meditation, as I like to describe it, is shifting from the external world (all that my senses take in) to my internal world, and that is where, I have discovered, my true essence lies. The practice makes me more attuned to my own inner voice and wisdom, increases my mental clarity and focus, and allows me to tap into what is often referred to as universal life energy, or chi, that which sustains and connects us all. It also keeps me calmer. On days that I forget to meditate or don't make time for it, I often become aware of a sense of anxiety or nervousness welling up inside of me, and I know I am not at my best.

Meditation remains a part of my daily routine, although I practice it only once per day on most days. At the very least, I take a minimum of five to ten minutes early in my day (and during the day as necessary) for meditation, prayer, and contemplation to center myself. This "grounding" brings me into the present moment rather than projecting into the future, obsessing about the past, or overreacting to little things throughout the day.

I eventually created a "meditation altar" on the top shelf of a low bookcase in a spare bedroom. It consists of a beautiful crocheted dresser scarf; some shells, stones and bits of nature I have collected; a candle; and other favorite objects. This serves as a sacred place for me to meditate, pray, read, journal – a spiritual resting place to connect with self and spirit. It also serves as a physical reminder of my spiritual practice. Pema Chödrön, a Buddhist teacher, says it is through spiritual practice that we learn to make friends with ourselves and our lives.

To keep my practice strong, I occasionally use guided meditation recordings, participate in group meditation classes in my community, and attend weekend-long meditation retreats. All of the above serve to support and deepen my practice.

The morning after my first Reiki session, I also had an internal desire to eat healthy and less. This was not a conscious decision. I emailed the practitioner about it and she explained that I now had a higher vibration and that heavy, unhealthy foods had a lower vibration. Vibrations, chakras, third eyes, Reiki, meditation . . . what was happening to me? I could only think of that iconic movie line from The Wizard of Oz: "Toto, I don't think we're in Kansas anymore." And just like Dorothy, I was entering a strange but beautiful new world, one where I would ultimately find my own truths.

I was becoming what I call "spiritually enthusiastic." I began reading anything I could get my hands on by spiritual teachers such as Wayne Dyer, Marianne Williamson, Sonia Choquette, and others. I attended lectures and weekend workshops on meditation and spirituality and personal development. Again, I had made no conscious decision to do all of these things collectively. It was like a spiritual magnetism pulling me forward. Author Marianne Williamson says that enlightenment is a shift from body identification to spirit identification. Could this be the path I was on? As in the quote sometimes attributed to Paolo Freire, "We make the road by walking," I was creating my new path with each step I took.

At the gift shop in the gym (paving stones to the spiritual pathway can be found in the most unexpected ways and places), I found a book by life coach and energetic healer Aleta St. James, titled *Life Shift*. The title grabbed my attention because it described, in two words, what I was experiencing. She describes a life shift as "[taking] your everyday life to the next level, where you can finally get rid of the emotional, mental, and physical obstacles that are holding you back." I could relate to all of this. Thank goodness for wonderful writers like the women and men I mention in this book, and others who have found their voices and are able to articulate their own experiences so those of us who feel confused and lost can read them and say, "Ah, yes. That is exactly what I am experiencing."

My annual visit to Miraval, about two months after that first Reiki session, was perfectly timed. While there, I took classes on meditation, yoga, journaling, qigong (similar to tai chi), and more. This all helped to keep up the momentum and was like a double shot of spiritual espresso propelling me forward on my journey toward self.

During this same time frame, I learned about the Kripalu Center for Yoga & Health, located in the Berkshire Mountains of Massachusetts, and the Omega Institute for Holistic Studies, in New York State, both educational retreat centers that I chose to visit. One facility is a former Jesuit seminary and the other a former children's summer camp. The accommodations are clean and comfortable, although very basic, quite the opposite of my beloved Miraval. However, both do offer massage and related "spa" services and therapies, not to mention beautiful settings. Both are a haven for self-discovery, healing on every level, and spiritual growth and development. They typically offer weekend or weeklong programs led by spiritual teachers, authors, and healers.

These facilities (and others like them) usually serve vegetarian meals, and while that can be a challenge for the uninitiated, sometimes it is good to simply try new things or do things differently than you are accustomed to doing them, even for a few days. It can make you more aware of what you're eating or introduce you to a new way of life. I found interesting workshops to attend, either by myself or with a friend, at each center. These trips served to further my spiritual awakening through education and practice, and act as a booster shot to maintain my ongoing spiritual health. Just as I did with Miraval, I now offer programs at Kripalu with a desire to guide others on their journey.

I'm not sure when I was first introduced to yoga, but I once purchased a yoga video to watch at home It was a good instructional piece, and I would periodically do the poses to the best of my ability. Over the years I took occasional yoga classes. I am far from your classic flexible willowy yoga devotee. In fact, most of it is quite challenging for me. But I learned that yoga, like meditation, is a discipline, something to be practiced. It is a very personal practice. I also eventually learned that there are many different styles of yoga practice, including chair yoga, that don't require twisting and bending and contorting. I have incorporated some simple yogic stretches into my daily routine that I also use any time in the day when I need an energy boost – they are things I can do almost anywhere, in whatever clothes I am wearing, and without getting on the ground! They help to focus my mind, and provide a time/space for silence, whether I do the practice alone or in a group. Yoga practice, even simple poses, requires concentration and focus. This makes it hard to think about other things, thereby giving me a break from my own mind. Like meditation, yoga gets me out of my head and into my body.

My husband, another light source on my journey, also contributed to my awakening. He is an artist, having painted in oils for over thirty years, and sees the world through artist's eyes. Joe taught me to "see" in a new way. While I would previously simply see a tree, a car, or a house, Joe sees shades of colors, shadows, and shapes. He notices texture, dimension, and depth in the world. He looks at something and sees all aspects of it, appreciating its uniqueness. Early in our marriage Joe would often call me to the window, exclaiming, "Come look at this!" I would initially feel annoyed that he was pulling me away from something terribly "important," like doing the dishes, but would dutifully go and look at whatever he wanted to share with me. He might comment enthusiastically, "Look at how the sun is reflecting on that tree, creating so many different shades of gold and green and brown." Slowly I began to see the complexity and beauty that he saw, and the world became much more vivid to me. I was becoming more aware of my surroundings and really being present rather than glazing over everything or whizzing by the scenery like a fast-moving train. Novelist Marcel Proust said, "The real voyage of discovery consists not in seeking new landscapes but in having new eyes."

As I was acquiring this new perspective and sense of awareness of myself and my relationship to the world, I also became aware of losing interest in and attachment to certain other aspects of my life. I once heard someone say that up until the age of fifty we work toward accumulating things, while after age fifty we work on getting rid of things. In that vein, I was experiencing a sense of wanting to let go . . . let go of emotional baggage from the past – old hurts and resentments, behaviors and reactions that no longer served me, and yes, even some of my material possessions and my excess body weight. I was asked to give a presentation to student nurses that year about wellness and holistic healing, and after doing some research, my core message for them – and in the process, for myself – was that in order to be an effective healer you must work on your own healing – body, mind, and spirit. Healing takes place on many different levels. I view it as working toward wholeness.

On a long car ride one day, I listened to *The Power* by Rhonda Byrne on CD. It is similar to her classic *The Secret*, but told in a slightly different way. Her core message, as I received it and interpreted it that day, was that only love matters. In other words, anger, jealousy, resentment, and regret serve no useful purpose. Love is the only thing that has meaning and therefore is what we should focus on: love for self, love for others, love from others, and love for life itself. So while driving, I made a decision to forgive everyone who had ever hurt me in the past – even those I might not remember. I also decided to forgive myself for all the things I did or didn't do that I felt bad about. What a powerful point to come to! This is not something that happened all of a sudden or just from listening to one CD. It was the right message at the right time, with me in a receptive mode and finally ready to let go of more of what was holding me back from living fully.

Forgiveness is part of the process of unburdening one's self. Yet forgiveness is not easy, partly because it is misunderstood. I heard the best explanation from a Buddhist meditation teacher when she said that forgiveness doesn't have anything to do with the other person, it has to do with you. In other words, forgiveness does not excuse or condone the act or event − which might have been awful − or the other person(s). Rather, forgiveness is about your ability to let what happened go and move on, to not let it hold you captive, thereby preventing you from living in the present moment. When we hold onto pain and hurt from the past, that pain keeps us prisoner.

I started to turn away from the past and look directly at the present and into the future. I was realizing that the past no longer mattered − not what happened to me or what I did. All that mattered was today and this moment. Now I could get on with my life with a new sense of joy and enthusiasm.

We have to get rid of that which holds us back and hides our true nature − negative and counterproductive habits and thought patterns − to make way for new energy, new ideas, new life. We need to drop ballast to be able to sail freely. We must let go of the past in order to fully embrace the future.

All along this new journey I was hearing and reading frequent references to Buddhist philosophy. I became intrigued and embarked on a course of self-study to learn more about it, not as a religious practice, but as an approach to life. This ongoing study has given me a more practical and realistic approach to both life and death.

Like Sleeping Beauty, I felt as though I was waking up from a very long slumber. But rather than waiting for a prince to arrive, I enrolled in graduate school. That sparked my intellectual awakening, which in turn paved the way for my spiritual awakening. And as the Chinese proverb goes: When sleeping women wake, mountains move!

LESSONS LEARNED

1. We always make time for those things that are truly important to us.

2. Where there is a will, there is always a way.

3. Help and support of all types are everywhere if you just seek them out.

4. If you don't ask, the answer is always no.

5. Education is a gift you give yourself. Higher education makes you a better version of yourself.

6. There are times when you have to trust the process and open yourself up to things that you may not yet understand.

7. Sometimes you have to just show up for life. That's when the magic happens.

8. You have to drop ballast to be able to sail freely.

9. We have to let go of the past in order to fully embrace the future.

RECOMMENDED READING

Arrien, Angeles. *The Second Half of Life: Opening the Eight Gates of Wisdom.* Boulder, CO: Sounds True, 2005.

Batchelor, Stephen. *Buddhism Without Beliefs: A Contemporary Guide to Awakening.* New York: Riverhead, 1997.

Byrne, Rhonda. *The Power.* New York: Atria, 2010.

Lesser, Elizabeth. *Broken Open: How Difficult Times Can Help Us Grow.* New York: Villard, 2004.

Tolle, Eckhart. *A New Earth — Awakening to Your Life's Purpose.* New York: Penguin, 2007.

RESOURCES

Kripalu Center for Yoga & Health www.Kripalu.org

Omega Institute for Holistic Studies www.eOmega.org

c h a p t e r   s i x

MAKING FRIENDS
WITH FEAR

Ultimately we know deeply that the other side
of every fear is freedom.
—MARY FERGUSON

FEAR HAS BEEN A CONSTANT COMPANION THROUGHOUT MY
life. It's not that I feel fearful every minute of the day. But
each time I am in an unfamiliar situation, trying something for the first time, setting a big goal, or stretching
myself in some way, fear comes a-callin', or more like a-
screamin'.

One of my earliest recollections of facing my fears
was at the age of eight, when my mother enrolled me in
swimming lessons at the local high school. I loved being
in the water and looked forward to my weekly sessions.
But once I mastered the basic skills, I was required to
jump off the diving board in order to advance to the next
level of competency. Although I could swim, I had a para-

lyzing fear of walking out on the diving board and jumping into the deep end of the pool. The thought of being thrust in way over my head gave me a deep sense of dread and being out of control. I imagined myself a blindfolded and bound pirate's prisoner walking the gangplank. So I had two choices: either refuse the challenge and therefore not advance in the swimming class, or force myself (in a good way!) to walk that plank and plunge into the unknown.

In the week before my next class, I weighed my fear of jumping versus the feelings of disappointment, embarrassment, and regret I would inevitably experience if I did not jump. Even at the young age of eight, I realized that my desire to advance in the class was stronger than my abject fear of jumping. This is what it often comes down to when I'm able to push through one of my fears: something even bigger than the fear pulling me forward. To prepare, I rehearsed a scenario in my mind where, in one fluid movement, I would walk to the edge of the diving board, hold my nose, pray, and jump in. In other words, I decided I had to get it over with quickly and hope for the best.

I did just that. In my one-piece faded swimsuit and bare feet, I emerged from the locker room onto the cool, damp tiles of the pool deck. You could probably see (and hear) my heart beating against the nylon of my suit as my anxiety grew. In the background I heard the echoing sounds of children's voices and water splashing, and the distinctive scent of chlorine entered my nostrils. I fixed my gaze on the diving board at the far end of the Olympic-sized pool as if spotting a big game animal in the sights of a shotgun. With fearful determination I moved toward the board, careful not to slip on the slimy surface, and lined up with others in my class as we got ready for the big jump. I watched as they, one by one, did what we came to do. The voice in my head was asking, *Are you sure you want to go through with this? You can still back out. Just say you have to use the restroom and don't come back – easy as pie.* I glanced nervously at the exit door. But before I could raise my hand to make such a request, it was my turn. So, getting swept up in the momentum of the moving line, and wanting desperately to be like everyone else in the class, I climbed the ladder, walked to the edge, held my nose and prayed, and while holding hands with my own fear, leapt in feet first. I miraculously made my way back up to the surface, swam to the edge of the pool, and hoisted myself out – still in one piece and breathing on my own. Instead of holding me back or not showing up at all, fear had come along with me, and together we had gotten the job done.

I walked back toward the shallow end of the pool, where the class would continue, with a slight smile on my face and took a very deep breath. I had a great sense of relief, satisfaction, and accomplishment. My fear and I had pushed me forward not only in the swimming class but in my own personal development, and I now felt a little braver, a little more confident, and a lot happier. And as often happens when we're afraid to do something,

I had realized that my fear of doing this thing was much worse than actually doing it. This experience has become a metaphor for my life. To this day I call on that "technique" when I have something scary to do. Mentally I "hold my nose, pray, and just jump in," with fear right beside me. Mark Twain said, "Courage is not the absence of fear. It is acting in spite of it." The diving board challenge was the first of many occasions when I would have to confront my fears and move forward in spite of them.

Fear is a powerful human emotion and can keep us from doing the things we want to do or ever finding out what we're truly capable of. I discovered, well into adulthood, that even successful and seemingly confident people face fear in their everyday experiences. They've just managed to keep moving forward in spite of it. But many of us become trapped by fear. I once heard someone say, "We are like prisoners in a cell where the jailer is gone and the door is open." This conjures up an image of the self-imposed "prison" many of us put ourselves in even though we're free to move forward at any time. We remain "trapped" or frozen in place. Fear becomes our jailer. Motivational speaker Les Brown said, "Too many of us are not living our dreams because we are living our fears."

Part of the problem, as I see it, is that there are two types of fear: the type you experience when walking down a dark alley at night in an unsavory part of town, and then the type we all experience when we are stepping outside of our comfort zone. Both types of fear serve a purpose — the first is to warn us of danger and keep our senses alert to protect us. The second type is a reminder that we are moving into new territory and need to stay alert to learning, which is a good thing. I refer to this type of fear as "growing pains." The problem is that we sometimes confuse the latter type of fear with the former. For example, I heard a woman who was doing something she had always wanted to do but feeling nervous about it say, "Hopefully being scared isn't some self-preservation alarm that I'm ignoring!" We're accustomed to backing off when feeling fear of any type and so have a hard time moving forward in the face of "growing pains" fear. How can you know the difference? Reflect inward and connect with the source of your unease. If your fear is that you might fail or not be good at something, that is "growing pains" fear. The other type is when "something just doesn't feel/seem right." Listen to your inner voices and instincts. The answers you seek are within you if you just take time to listen. This is part of getting to know yourself.

Fear is automatically part of the equation when you are challenging yourself. If you don't feel fear, you're not stretching yourself. The good news is that fear starts to dissipate after you do something for the first time or begin to master a new skill. You realize that the world will not stop spinning on its axis, or that you will not be vaporized by some cosmic laser gun if you act in spite of the fear. And, of course, as one fear starts to shrink, another will likely take its place as you push yourself even further along beyond the boundaries of your comfort zone.

The comfort zone is like an invisible bubble around each of us where we feel relatively safe and at ease. It's a place that is familiar to us, where we know how to handle most situations that arise, and feel that we have some mastery over our environment. When we step outside of it to try something new, challenge ourselves, or make a change, we automatically feel nervous and anxious. But once we do something for the first time or master a new skill, we push out the perimeter of that bubble and have a larger space in which to move around more comfortably.

So why push those seemingly safe boundaries at all? Why not just stay put? Because the comfort zone is a danger zone. When you're in it, you're not learning. And if you're not learning, you're not growing. If you're not growing, you're stagnating. Think of what a stagnant pool of water looks and smells like; it's not a pleasant sight or smell. It's also not a pleasant place to be in life. When you cease to learn, you cease to live. Personal growth and change are hard and even painful at times . . . at least at first. On the surface, it seems easier to stay put in whatever comfortable (or uncomfortable) rut you might be in. But "staying put" dulls your senses, slows your life force, and zaps your confidence. Yet every time you step out of your comfort zone, you become a little braver, a little wiser, and a little better equipped to face the world.

Once I had decided to start the seminar business, I began to feel fear the likes of which I had never experienced before. I have since learned that the bigger the goal, the bigger the associated fear or "growing pains." And because the fear didn't seem to want to go away on its own (annoying, spiteful emotion that it is), I did as I had done when I faced the diving board, and adopted a mental attitude (coping strategy) of bringing it along as my "friend." I would say to the fear that threatened to swallow me whole, "Okay, you pain in the butt – if you're going to stay here and vex me, you may as well come along with me. Just walk (or jump) alongside me, but not in front of me, because I'm going ahead anyway." This was the same strategy I had used as a child at the swimming pool. I had to make fear my ally rather than my enemy in order to keep moving forward. I began to understand that it was an inevitable part of personal growth. Rather than resisting it, I began to simply accept it. In so doing, I lessened its power over me.

On the day of my first scheduled seminar, after everyone was signed in and seated, it was time to begin the presentation. A wave of panic engulfed me. After dreaming about this for ten years and preparing for eighteen months, I now had to deliver what I had promised. It felt as though my feet were nailed to the ground. I quickly weighed my options: I could cancel the seminar and give everyone a refund, which would mean that my business and my reputation would be ruined. Or I could do what I had come here to do and force myself (in a good way!) to present the seminar that twenty-five individuals came to hear. Writer Jay McInerney said, "Sometimes the difference between what we want and what we fear is the width of an eyelash." What that says to me is that our dreams and goals and desires are all part of the same package with fear. They can't be separated, and the former don't become reality without the latter being present.

I hoisted myself up from the registration table where I had been sitting and focused my gaze on the spot I would be speaking from. I visualized two hands pushing me, along with my fear, down the center aisle, and started to place one foot in front of the other. When I reached my destination, I turned to face my audience, introduced myself, and began to speak. I presented for the next six hours (I had never spoken that long before), with breaks, of course. I had no audiovisuals, no jokes or stories. I spoke in a monotone, and was not very animated, all due to nerves and inexperience. I simply did the best I could.

At the end of the day, even with my novice performance, I had a great sense of relief and accomplishment just for having gotten through it all. I handed out evaluation forms to the participants, asking them to rate the content of the seminar as well as my presentation skills. But I purposely didn't review them right away. I simply wanted to relish the experience of having just completed something that was very challenging for me, and more importantly, represented the fulfillment of a longtime dream. And while I would have loved for the evaluations to have been favorable, I knew that if they weren't, I could fix that. I could work to become a better speaker, I could enhance the seminar, and I could even create a new seminar or market to a new audience if necessary. In other words, if it wasn't perfect the first time around, I would continue to work to make it better.

At home that evening, I called my sister, who was eager to hear how the day went. I relayed to her, "I am a different person this evening than I was this morning just for having done what I did today. It pushed me into a new stratosphere of existence, and there is no going back." Once again I had moved with my fear and propelled myself forward in the process. And by the way, the evaluations were actually pretty good. Imagine if I had given everyone their money back because I was too scared to deliver. I would never have known how they would receive that material or what I was capable of. My fears would have magnified, and my world would have become smaller. My life force would have dimmed a little further, too.

I know so many people who have been offered opportunities to write, or speak, or get promoted, or even learn something new on their job. And even though they might have loved to do it, they turned it down out of fear. That is sad because they missed a chance to experience a little more of life and get to know themselves a little bit better. Author Sheila MacKay Russell wrote, "You shouldn't avoid new experiences. You should welcome them. In not accepting them when they're offered to you, you restrict your own thought and capabilities. You lose a part of yourself."

While being interviewed on a radio show recently, talking about the subject of fear, I mentioned that most people are afraid of both failure and success. The host asked, a bit surprised, why would someone fear success? I explained that with success comes responsibility. When you raise the bar in any aspect of your life, you then have to work a little harder to keep it up. Also, if you do start to slide back, the higher you climbed on the ladder, the further you have to fall, potentially causing a more serious "injury" to your ego, self-esteem, and confidence. So some people decide to stay on the bottom rung of the ladder to play it safe. But playing it safe is one of the most dangerous things you can do. As previously mentioned, it restricts your growth and diminishes your confidence.

A few years after giving that first seminar, I received a call from a nursing colleague. She had been contacted by a small publisher who was looking for someone to write a book for first-year nurses. She thought I might be interested, so she passed the lead on to me. Although I was accustomed to working with more experienced nurses, rather than new nurses, I at least wanted to hear more about the project. Just speaking on the phone to a "real" publisher was enough to make my heart race, my pupils dilate, and my breathing become quick and shallow. I could never have imagined myself in this situation. I had been doing some article writing, but a whole book? I didn't know if I was up to the task. I had to ask myself, *Should I stay on the bottom rung or consider climbing the ladder?*

After several phone conversations, I agreed to write the book and was sent my first publishing contract. Having no idea what should or shouldn't be included in one, I had an attorney friend look it over for me. We negotiated a few minor changes, and I penned my name on the dotted line with considerable anxiety.

I no sooner received the countersigned contract than I fell into a deep state of panic. What had I done? What had I gotten myself into? What was I thinking? What were *they* thinking? I had no idea how to write a book or if I even knew enough to create something of value. I later became aware of a proverb that goes: "Sometimes you have to jump off the cliff and build your wings on the way down." That's exactly what I did when I signed that contract, without realizing it at the time. Just like my earlier diving board experience, I was once again jumping feet first, this time in a figurative sense. *Hold your nose, pray, and jump in,* I reminded myself. To my annoying friend Fear I said, "Take my hand. We're going in. Geronimooooooooo!"

A few weeks later, though, I found myself paralyzed by fear and unable to write. Among other things, I was afraid of failure and looking foolish. There was no fear of success in this equation because I didn't see that as even a remote outcome. A friend, who knew I was writing articles but didn't know I was working on a book, sent me a copy of *Chicken Soup for the Writer's Soul,* and I began to read. There were anecdotes from successful and even well-known writers, all of whom had experienced rejection, harsh criticism, crippling fear, oppressive self-doubt, and unrelenting negative self-talk. The stories made me realize that my feelings were quite common and that many writers had started out exactly where I was. That calmed me down and enabled me to move with fear and begin to write the book. Once again I was acknowledging my old friend Fear as part of the process of stretching myself and moving forward, rather than waiting for (or expecting) it to leave before getting anything done. And since fear was, as I now realized, an integral part of self-growth, propelling me forward and helping me realize my dreams, I had to admit I was starting to feel some real affection for it. *The next time I saw it coming,* I told myself, *I might even try to welcome it.*

I never thought it would be easy to write a book, but I didn't realize just how hard it actually would be until setting out to do it for the first time. There was research, interviews, writing, rewriting, editing, and proofreading. Then there was cover design and layout discussions, testimonials to obtain, and an introduction, acknowledgements, and marketing materials to write. I agonized over every word on every page and both covers. I was second-guessing myself and feeling woefully inept and unqualified every step of the way. Every day I had to push myself to continue, no matter how hard it seemed. Of course, being contractually obligated with firm deadlines and potential penalties for not meeting those deadlines was a strong motivator! I eventually finished the book on schedule because I was too scared not to.

Today the book, *Your 1st Year as a Nurse: Making the Transition From Total Novice to Successful Professional*, is in its second edition, is required reading for students and new nurses in many healthcare facilities and schools of nursing, and has been translated into Korean. Plus, this small publisher was eventually acquired by what is now Penguin Random House. I could very easily have rejected this opportunity out of fear and self-doubt. If I had, you might not be reading this book right now. Why? Because once we start to pull away from challenges, our fears tend to magnify while our confidence tends to shrink, neither of which encourages growth.

Of course you can never know the outcome when you set out to write a book, or start a business, or take painting or piano lessons. We spend so much time and energy worrying how things will come out or if we'll be successful at something that we forget to simply bask in the experience of learning something new or trying our hand at something we might enjoy. But there is no failure in trying – only varied experiences. We learn something from everything we do, whether it turns out as we expected or not. Additionally, few people are good at anything when they first try it. You develop expertise and skill through experience and study and even coaching. How will you ever know what you're good at or what you enjoy doing if you don't try different things? There is great benefit and joy in just "doing."

It's important to note that you can't confront or overcome your fears until you are able to be honest with yourself about them. For example, after going to Miraval for many years, I'd tried most of the classes and activities at least once. I had, however, managed to avoid the so-called "challenge activities." These consist of exercises designed to physically and mentally challenge you, such as climbing to the top of a pole and jumping off (while harnessed and tethered), something akin to bungee jumping but even safer. I'd had a million excuses why I didn't "need" to do those activities, such as: I came to relax; I don't have to prove anything to myself; I haven't broken any bones in my body yet, so why start now?

But when I visited the resort the year of my sixtieth birthday, I finally had to face the fact that I was afraid of those activities, deeply afraid. I had always had a horrible fear of heights and was worried about getting hurt on the challenge activity courses (even though all the participants are incredibly safe and well protected). I had to ask myself whether there was any real danger of getting hurt or whether I was creating an "excuse" and inflating the "dangers" in my mind to avoid the activities. Upon further introspection, I realized it came down to this: I didn't know if I had the courage, stamina, physical strength, and agility to get through those activities. In other words, this was one of those "growing pains" fears. I was trying to make it into a "danger" fear by focusing on the potential physical harm, in spite of all evidence to the contrary, as a way to avoid it. To make matters worse, while I had deliberately avoided these activities for so many years, my fear of them had been expanding exponentially.

Additionally, as I was getting older, I noticed that I had started to become risk averse and fear more things, especially things that required physical challenge. This is common with the aging process. So I knew I had to face my fears head-on or allow my world to become smaller and smaller, and withdraw a little from life each time I resisted. Plus, as a so-called motivational speaker, I had to practice what I preached. I knew that taking risks and getting yourself out there was scary, but that it could also be exhilarating, just like my earlier diving board experience and presenting my first seminar. So one of my goals on that trip was to challenge myself both physically and mentally.

I signed up for zip lining and another activity called "desert tightrope," where you climb a tall ladder and step out onto a tightrope with overhead hanging ropes to grab onto for support, while tethered and in a safety harness. I chose the zip lining challenge because I was considering taking my grandsons zip lining but was afraid of doing it myself. I thought this would be a good way to test it out and feel more comfortable. What if the first time I did it I was with them and found I didn't have the nerve to jump off the platform or started to whimper or cry? What kind of example would I be to them?

The day of the scheduled challenge activities, a voice in my head kept saying, "You can still cancel. You don't have to do this. No one will ever know that you backed out." But of course I would know – and I realized that the longer I avoided these activities, the larger the fear would loom. There is a German proverb that says: "Fear makes the wolf bigger than it is." So I decided to try not to think ahead to the scheduled activity time, but to stay focused on what was happening in the present moment. It wasn't easy, but I knew it was the only way I could get through this.

Of course the instructors and other participants at a resort like Miraval are incredibly supportive, and, as mentioned, conditions are very safe. But I had to ask, just to further reassure myself, if anyone had ever died or been seriously injured during this activity. The instructors assured me that no one ever had. I studied their faces to see if they were telling the truth. It appeared they were, so I decided I would climb. But I let all of the seven other participants in the group go ahead of me so I could watch how they did and observe how the instructors managed the cables attached to the harnesses for further reassurance.

These challenge activities all took place in the middle of the desert on the outskirts of the property, beyond the developed section of the resort. Because it was late autumn, the natural landscape was barren and drab with various shades of brown and beige. Dirt blew up from the unpaved pathways and the occasional tumbleweed would roll by like you'd see on an old Wild West movie set. I checked for circling vultures overhead just in case. None were in sight. I followed the length of the forty-foot wooden telephone-type pole with my eyes, tilting my head back until I could see the top. When my neck was hyper-extended as far back as it would go, my eyes finally spied the cap. I gulped. *Don't think about it too much, Donna, or you'll lose your nerve,* I heard my inner voice whispering to me.

It was finally my turn and I began to climb. I had to alternate lifting one hand and foot to the next rung and hoisting the other foot and hand up to meet the first. This maneuver had to be repeated an endless number of times, or so it seemed, all the while not looking down or up. Each individual movement was a struggle. About halfway up, I began to feel very fearful and physically weary. I wasn't sure I could make it to the top. It just seemed too hard. I contemplated working my way back down, even though I would have felt like such a failure if I did, especially since the rest of the group had success-fully scaled the pole. When I glanced down and realized how high I already was, I knew that even the climb down would not be easy. I told myself that I had to persevere and make it to the top. So I decided to focus on only the next step, rather than the top of the pole. I said out loud to myself in a soft, reassuring voice, "One more rung, Donna. One more rung. Don't stop moving. You'll figure it out. You can do this," even though I didn't completely believe that. I just willed myself, step by step, to keep going. Eventually I got to the top and precariously stepped onto the platform.

The climb itself was physically and emotionally taxing. But the hardest part was yet to come. All eight of us huddled together in the middle of a wooden platform with no railing along the edge. It was a fairly windy day, causing the platform to sway slightly, which made matters even worse. I couldn't help wondering how old the structure was or when it had last been checked for termite damage or if we were exceeding the maximum weight limit allowed by law. Would that chocolate cake I had last evening after dinner put extra stress on the lumber beneath my feet? We were each in a body harness and helmet and linked to an overhead cable for safety, but that provided little reassurance in the moment.

The instructor now told us to line up in preparation for jumping off the platform, attached to the zip line, one at a time. *Excuse me?* We're forty feet up and my brain was saying to me, *Are you crazy? Didn't you learn anything when you worked in the ER?* But I, and all of us, was at the point of no return. There was now only one way down. I made a strategic decision to go second. I figured that I could observe someone before me yet not have to wait too long before my turn, allowing the wolf to grow bigger. The first person to go had a very hard time stepping off the platform. She was being coached and encouraged by the instructor and the rest of us as well. But it took what seemed like an interminable amount of time before she finally squatted slightly and let the harness engulf her in a seated position like sitting onto a hammock or canvas swing, lifted her feet up, and glided off the platform, letting gravity do its thing.

Now it was my turn. I shuffled gingerly to the edge of the platform and tried not to think about how high up I was. I decided to mentally "hold my nose, pray, and jump in," and glide off the platform exactly as the person in front of me had. If I hadn't observed her doing it first, I might still be standing there, being told to "just step off," which seemed so counterintuitive. The zip line ride itself was both thrilling and fun. I experienced a great sense of freedom flying through the air, the euphoric rush of adrenaline, and a fantastic – if brief – panoramic view of the desert and surrounding mountains. I felt like a heroic swashbuckler coming to save the day! The ride itself was over so quickly that I had to ask myself what I had been so scared of. I had a very similar experience, overall, with the other challenge activity I chose. I felt triumphant and exhilarated afterward, and ready to take on the world.

It's important to note that each of us has our own unique fears and passions. What's scary to me may be something another person relishes, and vice versa. For example, in my nursing practice I have worked, without trepidation, in emergency rooms and psychiatric hospitals where others wouldn't dare to tread. And yet, while I had a fear of zip lining, I know others who couldn't wait to have the chance, and thrive on the thrill of it. We each have to identify, even honor, and face our own fears.

The experience of doing the challenge exercises reminded me, once again, that I am capable of doing so much more than I give myself credit for, even physically. Plus it helped me to keep my adventurous spirit alive. Facing fear and trepidation in one aspect of your life can prepare you for future challenges, even of a different kind. Fear is going to be present in all challenging situations, but you have to coach yourself through it with positive self-talk, break it into smaller pieces by taking it "rung by rung," and make friends with it.

By facing challenges – and the related fear – we expand our world, just as we shrink it by avoiding them. Whether jumping off the diving board, zip lining, or presenting my first seminar, I could easily have chosen to back away from the challenge and not do anything. But as Dale Carnegie put it, "Inaction breeds doubt and fear. Action breeds confidence and courage. If you want to conquer fear, do not sit home and think about it. Go out and get busy."

It's only by challenging yourself, pushing yourself beyond those seemingly safe boundaries, and trying something new that you truly discover who you are, what you are capable of, and where you belong in the world. Life is to be lived, to be experienced, and to be enjoyed. To be a participant rather than a spectator – that is to be truly alive. I suspect that this was one reason why former president George H. W. Bush went skydiving annually on his birthday after his retirement. The day you stop living is the day you start dying.

I try to challenge myself on a regular basis, always with fear by my side. It keeps me in the game. It propels me forward. It makes me feel alive. So how do I manage the related stress and anxiety? I try to focus on the present moment and relish the experience of just doing, rather than being obsessed about the outcome. I meditate, pray, and journal to keep me centered and connected to my inner knowing. I expose myself to positive people and messages to keep myself motivated. I set goals that challenge and stretch me, then go after those goals "rung by rung." And just as Mary Ferguson implies at the beginning of this chapter, I have experienced more freedom as a result.

Fear is an ongoing part of being alive. Knowing this, acknowledge fear, face it, embrace it, and befriend it. Then move through it, around it, or with it. Just don't let it hold you back and stop you from moving forward. If you make fear your traveling companion on the road of life, oh the places you will go together!

LESSONS LEARNED

1. Often the fear of doing something is much worse than actually doing it.

2. You only have to do something for the first time once. After that, it gets easier.

3. The answers you seek are within you, if you just take time to listen.

4. If you don't feel fear, you're not stretching yourself.

5. The comfort zone is a danger zone because when you're in it, you're not learning.

6. When you cease to learn, you cease to live.

7. The bigger the goal, the bigger the fear.

8. There is no failure, only varied experiences.

9. Taking risks and getting yourself out there is scary, but it can also be exhilarating.

10. Facing fear and trepidation in one aspect of your life can prepare you for future challenges, even of a different kind.

11. By facing challenges and the related fear, we expand our world rather than shrinking it by avoiding them.

12. The day you stop living is the day you start dying.

RECOMMENDED READING

Jeffers, Susan. Feel the Fear . . . and Do It Anyway. New York: Random House, 1987.

Nhat Hanh, Thich. Fear: Essential Wisdom for Getting Through the Storm. New York:

HarperCollins, 2012.

chapter seven

REBIRTH, REINVENTION, AND RESILIENCE

I should indeed like:
1) to begin again . . .
2) to begin again . . .
3) to begin again . . .

—COLETTE, QUOTED IN SECRETS OF THE FLESH: A LIFE OF COLETTE, BY JUDITH THURMAN

I MET A WOMAN A FEW MONTHS BACK WHO TOLD ME THAT she was turning fifty soon. "Congratulations!" I proclaimed. She looked at me as if I was crazy and uttered in a disgusted tone, "What's to celebrate? I feel so old." Since she was obviously in need of some encouragement, I assured her, "Fifty is a great age. Young enough to do absolutely anything you want and old enough to have amassed a good deal of wisdom and experience to leverage for your future." She looked as startled as if she'd just been hit with a stun gun. So for extra impact, and to leave her with food for thought, I added: "Fifty can be a time of rebirth for women or a time of decline – the choice is entirely yours." She clearly had never considered this perspective.

What I said to this woman applies to any situation in our lives. Whether turning forty or fifty or sixty or seventy, finding oneself a single woman after years of marriage, becoming an empty nester, being diagnosed with a life-altering illness, or losing a job, there is always an opportunity to move in a positive new direction with your life. You have to make a choice either to focus on the downside of any situation, and what you perceive you have lost, or on the chance to create something new from where you are.

Of all the challenges women face over their life span, age seems to be one of the biggest stumbling blocks for many. Over the years of writing an advice column for nurses, I would regularly get questions that started, "Dear Donna: Am I too old to . . . " and the rest of the sentence would be anything from "go back to school" to "start a business" to "change specialties" to "write a book," and more. These would come from individuals as young as twenty-eight who were already feeling "old." It's amazing how quick some of us are to send ourselves out to pasture. Last time I checked, none of us had a "use by" date stamped on the bottom of our feet. That's because there is no expiration date for living a full life, following your dreams, starting over, taking on a new project, or setting new goals. In fact, with today's ever-increasing life expectancy, most of us will live to be a ripe old age. And with the advances that have been made in research and science, in all likelihood we'll also be healthier and more active for the duration if we tend to our own self-care. So when I suggest to a woman that she go back to school or pursue a new career or start a new life after forty or even after eighty, the response I often get is: "But what if I don't live that much longer?"

My reply to that is always: "But what if you live to be a hundred? What will you do with the rest of your life?"

Previous generations, those born prior to the mid-twentieth century, had a fairly clear-cut model for their life: work or raise a family, retire in their sixties or seventies if they lived that long, and then downsize, scale back, and slow down. But everything is different today. Not only are we all living longer, most of us don't want to slow down and cut back as we age. We want to remain engaged in life, continue to enjoy activities and plea-sures, stay healthy and active. This doesn't mean that any of us has to keep working at a full-time job indefinitely, although for some of us that is exactly what we want or need to do. I hear many women say, "I have no plans to retire." That is either because they enjoy what they're doing, want to maintain a certain lifestyle and therefore want to keep their income up, or don't know what they would do with themselves if they did retire.

The word "retire" is being redefined in our society. I even heard someone suggest that the word will eventually be taken out of the dictionary because "no one is retiring anymore." Eleanor Roosevelt said, "When you cease to make a contribution, you begin to die." That's probably why so many men from previous generations died within a year of retiring. When we no longer feel useful, we begin to wither away. This highlights the importance of always staying active in a meaningful way, whether through employment, self-employment, volunteer work, helping out in some way – be it neighbors, family, the community, etc., mentoring, or coaching. Even someone who is homebound or disabled can help in various ways via phone, computer, or other means. When you give of yourself, life has meaning.

While speaking at a women's conference a few years ago, I talked about the fact that people are living and working longer and having a renaissance of sorts at every stage of life. Afterward a woman from the audience, probably in her late sixties, came up to me looking very relieved and elated, proclaiming, "Thank you for giving me permission to continue to live my life! My husband has recently retired and he wants me to retire too, but I don't want that lifestyle. It would kill me. I want to keep on doing what I'm doing for as long as I can. I love my career!"

My point is simply that as long as we are still alive, there is a lot of living to do. Our bodies, our minds, or our relationships may not be perfect, but that's no reason to stop learning new things, having new adventures, starting a new job or business, or forming new relationships. In fact, every day is an opportunity to get a fresh start. There are stories in the news weekly about a hundred-year-old man who ran a marathon, an eighty-year-old nurse still working in the operating room, a sixty-year-old woman swimming the English Channel, an eighty-five-year-old man getting his high school diploma, and ninety-year-old couples getting married. And consider the fact that Grandma Moses, the famous American artist, didn't start painting in earnest until the age of seventy-eight. As actress Olympia Dukakis's character in the movie *Moonstruck* notes (while quoting Yogi Berra), "It ain't over till it's over!"

Each decade of life has its own challenges, rewards, and opportunities. But reinvention and rebirth are not just about age. Many of us are thrown into situations at various stages of life where we need to retool, regroup, and reboot. Following are a few real-life women who had change trust upon them and learned how to adapt:

Helen, a homemaker her entire life, became a widow at the age of eighty-five when her husband of sixty-five years died after a protracted illness. Afraid of how she would carry on alone since she had spent so much time with her husband all those years, she resolved to stay social and not feel sorry for herself. After an initial grieving period, she decided to take up bowling and bocce. She also started to attend exercise classes for seniors, take local group trips, and volunteer on community committees and projects. These were all things she'd never had the time or the freedom to do as a family caregiver. On days when she doesn't have anything social planned, she goes into her well-worn cookbooks – a source of comfort for her – and looks for something to cook or bake that she can share with others. In these ways, she is never alone. She has created a new life for herself as a single woman.

Pat, a fifty-four-year-old professional photographer, suffered a serious hit to her business as the result of a depressed economy. During the same time period, she lost both of her parents within seven months of each other. "I always believed that I had complete control over my life," she says. "I suddenly realized that was not true, as things in my own life were spinning out of control." She had to give up her beloved business studio and look for photography work in the commercial sector, rather than the personal portrait work that she had previously relied on. She eventually realized that giving up the studio, as hard as it had been, lifted a lot of her financial stress and freed her to have more time for herself, for professional association involvement, and eventually for her son when he later became seriously ill. She advises, "Sometimes you have to find the strength to let go of the path you were on and have the patience to wait and see what comes next. If you don't accept that what you planned isn't what you've been given, you're just going to keep up the struggle. I feel as though I have been reinventing myself my entire life."

Julie Ann, at the age of fifty-nine, decided to give up her thirty-year career working in the financial services industry as an accountant because she lost interest in it. She opted to start her own business and a new career as a speaker, trainer, and coach. Drawing from her own work experience, she wanted to help companies and corporations create positive and productive work environments. She also became a Certified Laughter Leader, a designation that prepared her to use what's known as "therapeutic humor" in her programs. A year later she decided to end her unhappy marriage, and moved from a five-thousand-square-foot home to one only nine hundred square feet. "It was a big adjustment, and I'm still getting used to it," she says. But she claims that laughter, gratitude, and perseverance have helped her get through it all. She has no regrets about any aspect of her life and loves what she's currently doing. She adds, "The learning never ends."

Marilyn, a fifty-four-year old college professor with a PhD, had been a battered wife for fourteen years, something she long hid from the world. After an incident that finally made her realize that her son was a victim too, and with the advice of some friends in law enforcement, she was able to convince her abuser to leave the home that she had owned before they were married, under threat of legal action. "Hiding doesn't help," she admits, "but you have to know who to reach out to. I decided I was no longer going to be pulled down into the gutter with him." She was now a single parent with substantial debt that she is still paying off eight years later. "I was fortunate that I had a good job and knew that

I could also do freelance work if necessary to get by," she says. She eventually learned to stop being scared to death by controlling the few things that she could throughout the process, including indulging in creative writing, practicing gratitude, and nurturing friendships. "My weight had ballooned while I was married, so I joined a weight-loss program and found a supportive community there. I also started walking five miles each day." Additionally, Marilyn focused on helping others in any way she could, whether sharing a meal, a toy, or some flowers from her garden. "Giving made me feel good," she explains. Today she works with displaced homemakers to help them get back on their feet after abuse, hardship, and loss.

Julie Mae was thirty-nine, happily married, and the mother of two young children when she was diagnosed with breast cancer. She says that when she had to endure a grueling year of chemotherapy and radiation, a valiant person stepped forward from within her. "I learned a lot about human nature during that time. I was the one undergoing chemo, but I observed that most people, while healthy, are just walking zombies." After treatment ended, a new, emboldened person emerged, one who is unapologetic, less cautious, and less of a people pleaser. "I don't feel I need to explain myself to anyone anymore," she says. "I can be more authentic in who I am and the choices I make for my life. I came out of the ordeal wiser and more mature and even appreciative of the experience." With a background in computer technology, she is now planning to do some motivational speaking and write an inspirational book. Her core message: dream without reservations, and take action without hesitation.

These are just a few examples of women who had to create a new model for their lives and careers when circumstances forced their hands. Rather than focusing on their losses or their troubles, they created new plans, adopted new attitudes, and took steps to move through their challenges to a new phase of life. In so doing they have made themselves stronger to face future challenges and changes, and learned something about themselves.

These women were also practicing resilience: the ability to bounce back after tragedy, recover quickly from difficulties, not stay a victim, and adapt more easily to change. When life knocks you down, resilience is the ability to get up stronger. Rather than let perceived failure overcome them and drain their resolve, resilient people find a way to rise from the ashes, again and again. And while resiliency comes more naturally to some, the psychological community says that it can be learned and developed. How? By building a strong social community, finding a purpose in life, always having goals to work on, practicing gratitude, being flexible, continuously learning something new, staying positive and optimistic, nurturing yourself, creating a spiritual practice, embracing change as a natural part of life, building a positive sense of self, and always challenging yourself.

Resiliency is especially important today because we live in a time of great change and global instability. Plus, the longer we live the more challenges and opportunities for starting over we will experience. So it is an especially important trait as we age, but should be cultivated at every time in our lives.

An example of a remarkable resilient spirit is Bethany Hamilton, a young woman who, while surfing, lost her left arm during a shark attack in 2003. Her case was highly publicized, not only because of the incident but because three weeks later she got back on her surfboard and hit the waves again. She made numerous TV appearances at that time. During one such interview, after she left the stage, the hosts were perplexed at how she could be so upbeat about her situation so soon after the accident. They even speculated that perhaps she was still in shock.

What the interviewers failed to realize was that Bethany had made a conscious decision to accept her "new normal" and get on with her life rather than wallow in her loss. I'm sure she went through an initial grieving process, but she was able to move past it. She adjusted by teaching herself how to surf with one arm, learning new ways to stay balanced on the board. She even went on to be victorious in the world of professional surfing. Ten years after the attack she was in the news again because she was getting married.

I recently read *Finding Me* by Michele Knight, one of three young women who were held captive and brutalized by one man for over ten years in an Ohio home. The story is horrific and it is difficult to understand how any of these women could have endured such an experience. Michele also suffered for twenty years prior at the hands of abusive and neglectful relatives. But Michele came out of the ordeal with a sense of gratitude for having survived. She also believes that she was meant to help others who have suffered similarly, and advocate for those still being held captive somewhere. It is a story of triumphant and amazing resilience. I hesitated to read it, worried that I wouldn't be able to process her tale of horror. But the book doesn't focus on the abuse she suffered. Instead it is uplifting and illustrates how she not only survived thirty years of abuse, being homeless, and losing custody of her son, but how resilient the human spirit can be. In the end, she is happy to be free and alive. She refuses to remain a victim any longer.

Every one of us has our own stories to tell, our own challenges to face, our own history to overcome. But as the old adage goes, it's not what happens to you but what you do with it that matters. Each of us will experience numerous losses in our lives. We can allow each loss to define us and suffer as a result, or we can accept what we cannot change and − like the women above − find a new way to achieve balance. We might even be able to be "victorious" in our own way, as Bethany the surfer was, within each "new normal" we encounter. Pain and loss are inevitable in life, but suffering is optional. We suffer needlessly when we deny rather than accept what is. The choice belongs to each of us.

For me, each decade of life has presented an opportunity to reflect on what I've done in the past and what I still want to accomplish. After turning sixty, having been self-employed for twenty years, I decided to make a lot of changes. I set out to completely reinvent and refresh my business with new programs and areas of focus and new ways of delivering my message. So I underwent a business makeover. After working almost exclusively with nurses and healthcare professionals for twenty years, I wanted to branch out to working with women from all walks of life. I felt a great deal of passion for this. I started to conduct retreats and workshops for caregivers, women in transition, and those who want to empower themselves to live a fully awake and enlightened existence.

But I had to give up some of the work I had been doing for twenty years to make room for new ideas, new ventures, and new energy. I decided to give up writing my five-day-a-week advice column for nurses, which I had done for fifteen years. I didn't make that decision lightly, since I was well known for my "Dear Donna" column, and it had been instrumental in building my brand as a nursing career expert. I also decided to stop doing full-day seminars, something I had launched my business with and had become known for in my original target market. That was also a big decision that took me a few years to make. And while it was difficult to let go of things that had been so much a part of my life and success for so many years, doing so opened up space in my schedule, my energy field, and my psyche to dream new dreams and devote time to new projects, including writing this book. It even allowed more time for me to enjoy life and family. This shift took a lot of planning and execution, but I feel incredibly reenergized by the process. It has given me a renewed zest for life and work. I am able to do more of what I love to do, with less of the tedium of my prior schedule and activities. I am looking toward the future. And if I can reinvent my business in my sixties as I plan the next twenty years and beyond, you can make the change you've been longing to make too, at any age. I, for one, am rooting for you.

The dandelion puff pictured on the cover of this book is very symbolic. At first glance, the transformed flower may seem to be falling apart and dying. But what's really happening is that the flower is regenerating itself. Each cottony thread, which is dispersed with the slightest breeze, is attached to a seed. But the seed must fall in order to grow. And that is a perfect analogy for how hard times foster our personal growth as human beings.

When I think back to where I was twenty years ago, when my husband got sick and everything in my life seemed to be falling apart, I can now see how each challenge and change made both of us stronger, more alive, more joyous, and even more grateful for the lives we now celebrate each day. In the end, everything is falling together just as it is supposed to.

RECOMMENDED READING

Levine, Suzanne Braun. *Inventing the Rest of Our Lives: Women in Second Adulthood.* New York: Viking Penguin, 2005.

Reivich, Karen, and Andrew Shatté. *The Resilience Factor: 7 Keys to Finding Your Inner Strength and Overcoming Life's Hurdles.* New York: Broadway Books, 2002.

ACKNOWLEDGMENTS

This book has been long in the making and would not have happened without the help and support of so many. So to the following people, I offer my heartfelt thanks and gratitude:

Brooke Warner, Cait Levin, and everyone at She Writes Press for their professionalism, guidance, and advice.

Katherine Sharpe, editor extraordinaire, for both pulling and pushing me in the right direction with my writing.

Marion Roach for the great advice, encouragement, support, and feedback.

Michael Tompkins, friend and colleague, for the ongoing help and support on this project and all of my work.

Marcia Blackwell, Julie Mae Stanley, Juanita Painson, Carol Walkner, Catherine Tansey, Linda Bremer, Barbara Davis, Amy Mallet, Melinda Salzer, Vicki Delaney, Lisa Foulke, and Michele Manegio – all extraordinary women in their own right – for editorial support, input, opinions, ideas, and feedback.

All the women and men who have shared their stories of triumph and tragedy with me over the years.

The countless fans, followers, clients, and colleagues who have asked for and encouraged me to write this book over the years.

Emily Kingsley for her gracious permission to allow me to reprint "Welcome to Holland," and all the wonderful work she does inside and outside of the disability community.

My amazing family who keep me laughing no matter what is going on in my life: David, Pia, Justyna, Junior, Sebastian, Helen, Rose, Barbara, Barry, Eddie, Nancy, Eugene, Linda, Pamela, Paul, Anna, Mimi, Andrew, Matthew, Lily, Max, and Jasper.

And especially to Joe, my husband and partner in everything I do, for his endless patience, unconditional love, pro bono editing and proofreading, exceptional culinary skills, and boundless inspiration.

ABOUT THE AUTHOR

DONNA WILK CARDILLO, RN, is The Inspiration Nurse – a transformational keynote speaker, humorist, retreat and seminar leader, and author helping others to be fearless in career and life and maximize their potential. Her accomplished career combines more than thirty years of clinical, managerial, and business experience, not to mention her stint as a professional singer! Her clinical experience includes emergency and psychiatric nursing. She blogs at DoctorOz.com and is the former Dear Donna columnist at Nurse.com and Monster.com. She is also a passionate advocate for family caregivers. Donna is a lifelong Jersey girl and lives at the beautiful Jersey Shore in Sea Girt, NJ, with her husband, Joe. Find out more at www.DonnaCardillo.com.

SELECTED TITLES FROM SHE WRITES PRESS

She Writes Press is an independent publishing company
founded to serve women writers everywhere.
Visit us at www.shewritespress.com.

*Where Have I Been All My Life? A Journey Toward Love and
Wholeness* by Cheryl Rice. $16.95, 978-1-63152-917-7. Rice's
universally relatable story of how her mother's sudden death
launched her on a journey into the deepest parts of grief – and,
ultimately, toward love and wholeness.

Think Better. Live Better. 5 Steps to Create the Life You Deserve by
Francine Huss. $16.95, 978-1-938314-66-7. With the help of this
guide, readers will learn to cultivate more creative thoughts,
realign their mindset, and gain a new perspective on life.

*The Thriver's Edge: Seven Keys to Transform the Way You
Live, Love, and Lead* by Donna Stoneham. $16.95, 978-1-63152-980-1.
A "coach in a book" from master executive coach and leadership
expert Dr. Donna Stoneham, *The Thriver's Edge* outlines a
practical road map to breaking free of the barriers keeping you
from being everything you're capable of being.

*Don't Leave Yet: How My Mother's Alzheimer's Opened My
Heart* by Constance Hanstedt. $16.95, 978-1-63152-952-8. The
chronicle of Hanstedt's journey toward independence, self-
assurance, and connectedness as she cares for her mother, who
is rapidly losing her own identity to the early stage of
Alzheimer's.

*Flip-Flops After Fifty: And Other Thoughts on Aging I Remembered
to Write Down* by Cindy Eastman. $16.95, 978-1-938314-68-1. A
collection of frank and funny essays about turning fifty – and all
the emotional ups and downs that come with it.

Four Funerals and a Wedding: Resilience in a Time of Grief by Jill
Smolowe. $16.95, 978-1-938314-72-8. When journalist Jill
Smolowe lost four family members in less than two years, she
turned to modern bereavement research for answers – and
made some surprising discoveries.

CPSIA information can be obtained
at www.ICGtesting.com
Printed in the USA
FSHW01n1956061018
52727FS